The FORGOTTEN ADVENTURES of *Richard Halliburton*

A High-Flying Life from Tennessee to Timbuktu

R. SCOTT WILLIAMS

Published by The History Press
Charleston, SC 29403
www.historypress.net

Copyright © 2014 by R. Scott Williams
All rights reserved

First published 2014

Manufactured in the United States

ISBN 978.1.62619.720.6

Library of Congress Control Number: 2014952246

Notice: The information in this book is true and complete to the best of our knowledge. It is offered without guarantee on the part of the author or The History Press. The author and The History Press disclaim all liability in connection with the use of this book.

All rights reserved. No part of this book may be reproduced or transmitted in any form whatsoever without prior written permission from the publisher except in the case of brief quotations embodied in critical articles and reviews.

To Michelle, Alex and Liv, the ultimate traveling companions.

Contents

Acknowledgements	7
Preface	9
1. In the Beginning, Brownsville	15
2. Mary Hutchison	24
3. Heartsick	27
4. Memphis to New Orleans and Beyond	34
5. Higher Education	39
6. Post Princeton	46
7. The Royal Road	53
8. Right Time, Right Place	57
9. Choking Destiny	65
10. Bobbs-Merrill	70
11. Drowning in the Hellespont	75
12. What the Public Wants	79
13. New Worlds to Conquer	90
14. Ladies' Man	100
15. Flying Carpet	104
16. Lights, Camera, India	122
17. Pinnacle of Success	128
18. Hangover House	133
19. The *Sea Dragon*	142

CONTENTS

Epilogue	159
Notes	171
Bibliography	179
Index	189
About the Author	192

Acknowledgements

First and foremost, thanks go to all those who have written so well about Richard Halliburton in the past, including John Alt, Michael Blankenship, James Cortese, Gerry Max, Chip Deffaa, Jonathan Root, Barbara Schultz, David Schwartz, William Taylor, Guy Townsend and many others. Much credit for this book goes to Kirsten Schofield for the idea and the encouragement.

Wesley Halliburton's dedication to archiving his son's life and accomplishments was invaluable, as was the access, permission and assistance generously granted by Bill Short and the team at the Rhodes College Archives, who have lovingly cared for and continued the collection Wesley Halliburton began. The help and access to the Bobbs-Merrill archives at the Lilly Library at Indiana University was greatly appreciated. Thanks to Sharon Naron at the Hutchison School; Sonia Outlaw-Clark, Lynn Shaw and the Halliburton family in Haywood County, Tennessee; and Rick Mastroianni at the Newseum in Washington, D.C. I am filled with gratitude for my wife and amazing proofer, Michelle, and my daughters, Alex and Liv, who responded with patience and understanding when I was in a library, out of town or locked away in the study.

A special thanks to all those journalists and photographers who shared Richard Halliburton's adventures with the world and all the writers in small towns and big cities who, in their own unique and individual styles, shared reviews of his books and personal appearances with the readers of their community newspapers.

Finally, this book wouldn't be possible without my large Haywood County family, who taught me how to appreciate a good story.

Preface

May 13, 1945
For six years the Pacific Ocean has kept locked in its depths the mystery of the fate that overtook Richard Halliburton, adventurer and writer, who disappeared when his Chinese junk, the Sea Dragon, *vanished midway between Hong Kong and San Francisco in March 1939. Speculation on the fate of Halliburton and his crew was revived the other day when the water-logged hull of a small vessel obviously of the same type as Halliburton's was washed ashore at Pacific Beach, near San Diego, Calif. Little remained of the ship, only a flat-bottomed section of heavy timbers, held together with huge brass bolts.*
—American Weekly

By the time remnants of what possibly was the *Sea Dragon* (but most likely wasn't) washed up on a beach near San Diego, California, on May 13, 1945, Richard Halliburton and the crew of the Chinese junk had been dead more than six years. During that time, the nation had been focused on fighting the Second World War, so by the time it was suggested a piece of Halliburton's boat had washed ashore, it wasn't the big news it would have been just a decade earlier.

Born in the very first days of the twentieth century, this son of the well-to-do cotton culture of West Tennessee eventually became the most-famous adventure writer of his day. Halliburton inspired millions of readers, young and old alike, to add a little travel and adventure to their lives. And because he lived from 1900 to 1939, his life and career was lived out against the backdrop of a world going through dramatic growth and change. With books on the bestseller lists for years at a time and selling well over a million copies, he made and spent huge sums of money during the Jazz Age and then the Great Depression. As a lecturer and radio personality, millions of individuals personally heard him share his stories in a unique style that was unlike anything anyone had ever heard before.

In his lifetime, Halliburton climbed Mount Olympus in Greece, the Matterhorn in the Swiss Alps and Fujiyama in Japan. He swam the length of the Panama Canal and plunged into the Hellespont in Turkey. He was arrested in Gibraltar, slept on top of the Great Pyramid in Egypt and was the first to photograph both Mount Everest and the Taj Mahal from the air. Halliburton rode a donkey over the Pyrenees and, in homage to Hannibal, rode an elephant across the Alps. He spent time with convicts on Devil's Island and a month on the island of Tobago pretending he was Daniel Defoe's Robinson Crusoe. Halliburton joined the Foreign Legion, dove seventy feet into a Mayan well of death at Chichen Itza and flew all the way from here to…yes, Timbuktu—literally, right across the middle of the Sahara Desert in an airplane he christened the *Flying Carpet*.

During that time, the articles about his adventures helped sell a lot of newspapers and magazines. When radio was still in its infancy, and before movie theaters sprang up around the country, Americans escaped the boredom of their everyday lives and explored the world around them through ink on paper. With a combined weekly circulation of nine million, Halliburton's syndicated articles appeared in newspapers around the country. While some critics rolled their eyes at his obvious tendency to embellish and an overly enthusiastic and youthful writing style, his fans flocked to hear him speak at public appearances, and teachers applauded him for bringing to life historic events and introducing young readers to the enjoyment that can be found in a good book.

Halliburton was also popular with the rich and famous. His friends included fellow adventurers, journalists, painters, writers, politicians, musicians and entertainers. Known for his unique sense of personal style, good looks and carefree attitude, it was good to have Richard Halliburton at your party. At the height of his career, his fame was equal to well-known personalities like Amelia Earhart, Charles Lindbergh, Charlie Chaplin, Rudolph Valentino and F. Scott Fitzgerald.

If you had been in Kansas City, Missouri, on September 11, 1927, you would have unfolded your copy of the *Kansas City Star* and read an editor's introduction to an article by Richard Halliburton that provides a great summary of the Halliburton image, especially at the beginning of his career:

> *Richard Halliburton typifies the romantic spirit of youth—the desire to do-and-dare, to fulfill dreams regardless of consequences, attempting feats*

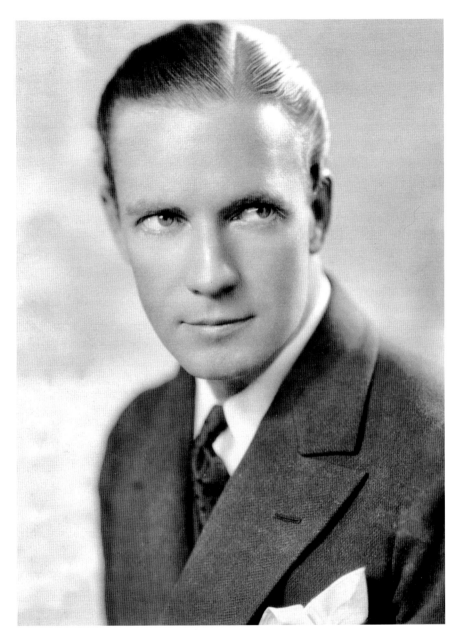

Autographed promotional photograph, 1929. *Courtesy of the Rhodes College Archives and Special Collections, Memphis, Tennessee.*

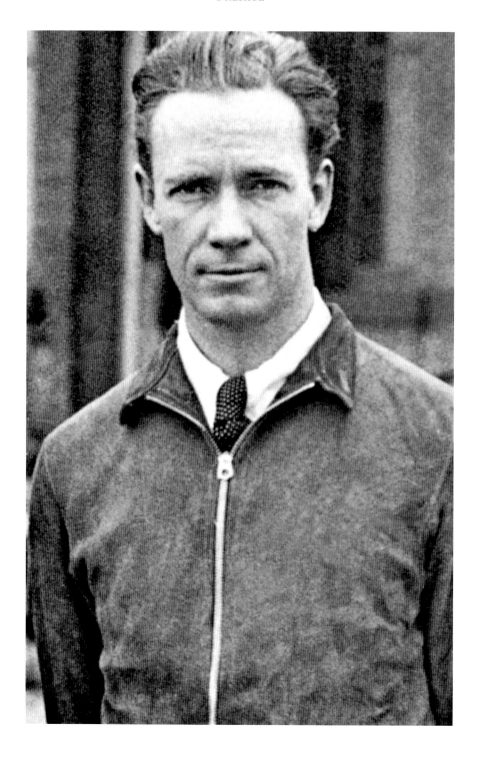

Preface

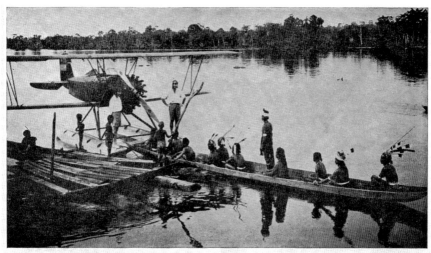

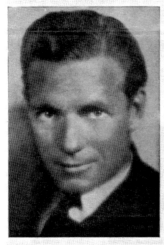

Flyer promoting a Richard Halliburton lecture. *Courtesy of the Rhodes College Archives and Special Collections, Memphis, Tennessee.*

Opposite: Richard Halliburton toward the end of his life. *Author's collection.*

that older heads have declared impossible. Seemingly throwing caution to the winds, he has experienced enough thrills to last a normal man a lifetime. A recent Princeton graduate and reared in most comfortable circumstances, he has lived the life of a vagabond in a tour of the world—brother to a prince and fellow to a beggar if he be found worthy.

Halliburton was among the first American personalities to create an entertainment brand and then perpetuate it in order to achieve validation, media attention and financial reward. While Charlie Chaplin became the "little tramp with a big heart," Amelia Earhart was the "female flyer making it in a man's world" and Charles Lindbergh was the "handsome daredevil," Richard Halliburton was the "boy adventurer" who, like Peter Pan, refused to grow up. The only problem was that when he grew tired of that image, he found it impossible to shake.

His last adventure, and the one that resulted in his death at age thirty-nine, took place on an ancient Chinese junk he had built in Hong Kong and was sailing with a crew to the Golden Gate International Exposition in San Francisco. In late March 1939, the crew of the *Sea Dragon* encountered a typhoon, and tragically, all aboard were lost. Although the expedition was driven by exhaustion, desperation and a misplaced sense of confidence, with a small shift in the weather or the timing, things could have turned out differently and Halliburton would have, once again, defied the odds. But this time, it didn't work out that way.

It's impossible to sum up Richard Halliburton's life in a neat little "happily-ever-after" package. Eventually, although he achieved great success, fame and pop-culture notoriety, he felt loved by very few, and his life became one of great contradictions. It's also difficult to understand how someone who became so famous could disappear so completely from history. For an article in *Smithsonian Magazine*, David M. Schwartz wrote, "He was Marco Polo and Indiana Jones wrapped up in one, with P.T. Barnum's flippancy and James Bond's bravado, capped off by F. Scott Fitzgerald's aristocratic good looks and manners."[1] In a 1977 issue of city *City of Memphis* magazine, Guy Townsend wrote, "Richard Halliburton was in his own way a remarkable man who lived an interesting and eventful, if incomplete, life; and for a decade and a half, anyway, he was the most famous Memphian in the world."[2] Those descriptions work well. But perhaps Halliburton's father, Wesley, described him best when, many years after his son's death, emotion cracking in his voice, he said, "Richard was a meteor…that blazed across the heavens…and was gone."[3]

CHAPTER 1

In the Beginning, Brownsville

October 13, 1935
Hanging onto a runaway horse by one foot for more than a mile when he was only five years old was the start of a life full of adventures for Richard Halliburton, Memphis writer and world traveler. He will speak at the Auditorium Wednesday night under the auspices of the Memphis Art Association.
—Commercial Appeal

Located in Haywood County, in the heart of the West Tennessee Delta, just sixty miles east of Memphis, is Brownsville, Tennessee. Officially founded in 1823, it had previously been the hunting grounds for Cherokee and Chickasaw Indian tribes. The soil was made especially fertile by Haywood County's proximity to the Hatchie River, so it made the perfect land on which to grow cotton and other crops, creating a strong, growing economy until the Civil War. Like other areas of the South, most of the settlers of West Tennessee were slave owners, and as they migrated to Haywood County, they brought their slaves with them to clear the area and create acre after acre of fertile farmland. In the aftermath of the Civil War, the cotton economy rebounded; however, the size of most farms was greatly reduced, and many of the "great, old Southern families" struggled to recover.

Richard Halliburton was a descendant of one of those great southern families. His grandparents John Wesley and Juliet Halliburton were distant cousins, both descendants of David Halliburton, who emigrated from Edinburgh, Scotland, to Philadelphia in the early 1700s. Eventually, a

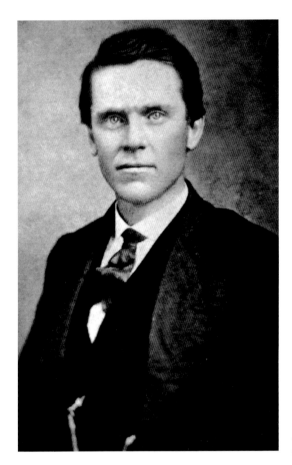

Richard Halliburton's paternal grandfather, John Wesley Halliburton, before 1872.
Courtesy of the Rhodes College Archives and Special Collections, Memphis, Tennessee.

branch of the family settled down in Haywood County and began farming hundreds of acres of land. They became wealthy enough that Richard Halliburton's grandfather John Halliburton was able to attend the University of North Carolina at Chapel Hill at a time when education for most of their Haywood County neighbors amounted to a few years in a one-room schoolhouse, if that.

While in college, John sent Juliet, who was his fiancé at the time, many romantic letters. In one, he wrote:

> *Darling please write at least once a week. I can't bear disappointment now. I have expected a letter from you every week. Don't disappoint me now my darling. Father never writes—I can't hear from home—then darling not to hear from you (equal to all the world) will be too bad. As long as you write*

to me I can bear up under all of Fortune's freaks. When you write all is joy and love—when you write I feel indipendent [sic] *of all the world. When you write Chapel Hill is bearable—be silent and the reverse is my doom.*[4]

In another letter, John described a "pro-Union" speech that he gave at a secessionist rally. He wrote, "I was taken up by some boys and rode around on their shoulders and they carried me to the ladies who gave me a Boquett [sic], but it was a secession boquett [sic] and could not sail under the 'Star Spangled Banner' pinned to my heart."[5]

Although he opposed secession, John Halliburton's loyalty to his family and community was greater, and he eventually enlisted in the Confederate army. He was visiting his fiancé in her hometown of Little Rock, Arkansas, when, following a brief gunboat battle below the Memphis bluffs on June 6, 1862, the Union army overtook the city and turned Memphis into a supply depot and staging area. John Halliburton enlisted with a Confederate regiment in Arkansas and eventually was captured and spent time in a Union prisoner of war camp. After the war, John and Juliet Halliburton married, and he began farming his family's land near the Forked Dear River in Haywood County. The couple had six children, with three sons living to adulthood: Garland Garrison, John Holloway and Richard Halliburton's father, Wesley.

In 1872, John Halliburton died, and Juliet moved back to her hometown of Dewitt, Arkansas, with Wesley and his two older brothers. She married William Stillwell, and they created a nice life for her three young boys. Years later, Wesley Halliburton referred to his childhood as "a wild, free, and open life, galloping over the prairies on my Texas mustang pony."[6] An article he wrote for a Memphis newspaper offers another small glimpse of his life in Dewitt:

I helped sing, with considerable zeal, at the once-a-month church services over in the…log church house, in Arkansas County. My mother would hold a song service at home on Saturday, to practice the hymns we would sing the next day. She didn't care too much for lining out the words or too long meter. This was one time I enjoyed going to church, and on account of my fondness for harmony, I would sing more bass to the bar than the script called for.[7]

At thirteen years old, Wesley Halliburton attended boarding school in Covington, Tennessee, and was there when he received word that his mother was ill. On October 11, 1883, before he could get home to say goodbye,

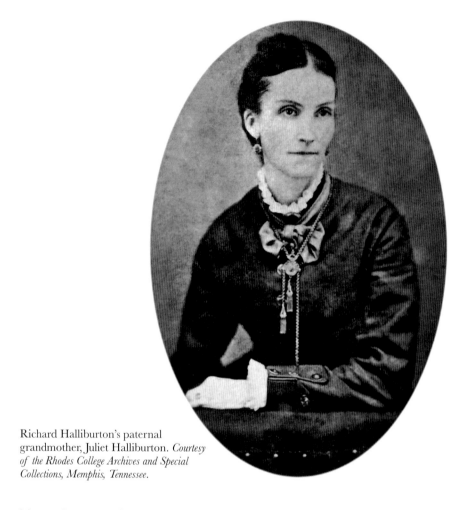

Richard Halliburton's paternal grandmother, Juliet Halliburton. *Courtesy of the Rhodes College Archives and Special Collections, Memphis, Tennessee.*

his mother passed away. Fortunately, he had a strong extended family and remained close to his older brothers and his maternal grandfather, Colonel William H. Halliburton.

Colonel Halliburton, an attorney, had been born on November 4, 1816, to Thomas and Lucinda Halliburton, who were from Tennessee by way of North Carolina. While living in Benton County, Tennessee, William Halliburton was elected colonel of the 113th Regiment of the Tennessee Militia. He moved first to Memphis and then to his final home in Dewitt, Arkansas, where he simultaneously held the positions of deputy clerk and deputy sheriff. When the Civil War began, Colonel Halliburton was appointed chief collector of the war tax for the state of Arkansas. After the war, President Andrew Johnson pardoned Colonel Halliburton so he could continue practicing law in the federal courts. Wesley Halliburton had fond memories of his grandfather, and he wrote:

> *Colonel Halliburton was a man of dignified bearing, nearly six feet tall, but weighing less than 200 pounds. He wore a Confederate grey Prince Albert suit and a medium white hat. In the summertime he pulled off his heavy coat, but had a long alpaca coat instead, as he would never be seen in shirtsleeves. He had blue eyes and medium dark hair. He belonged to the Baptist Church and was a man who practiced the tenants of the Bible in his daily life.*[8]

Colonel Halliburton compiled a history of Arkansas County and instilled in his grandson a love of reading, writing and history, which Wesley Halliburton would pass along to his own son, Richard.

After his mother's death, Wesley Halliburton was sent to a prep school in Fayetteville, Tennessee, and later attended Vanderbilt University in Nashville, Tennessee, where in 1891 he received a civil engineering degree with honors. Afterward, he attended the Massachusetts Institute of Technology in Boston and then spent some time working as an engineer for several firms in the area. He quickly grew tired of sitting behind a desk all day and returned to Haywood County to try his hand at farming the five hundred acres he had inherited from his father. He farmed the land with such success that he was asked to take over the management of several other troubled farms, which he also turned around.

Soon after moving back to Haywood County, and after a failed engagement to a local girl, Wesley met Nelle Nance, a young woman who had come to teach at the Brownsville Female College. She had been born in Paris, Tennessee, on March 9, 1869, to John and Amanda Blythe Nance. Nance had also experienced a childhood of loss. Her father died when she was three and her mother when she was thirteen. Relatives sent the young orphan to study piano at the Cincinnati Conservatory of Music, and after graduation in 1892, she became the head of the music department of the Athens Female College in Athens, Tennessee. Later, she accepted a similar position at the Brownsville Female College.

Nelle and Wesley Halliburton were married on a cold, rainy night at the Brownsville Methodist Church on January 19, 1898. The church was decorated with large amounts of mistletoe, and an article in the *Commercial Appeal* called their wedding "the handsomest affair of the kind ever witnessed." Afterward, a reception was held at the college. The young couple was well

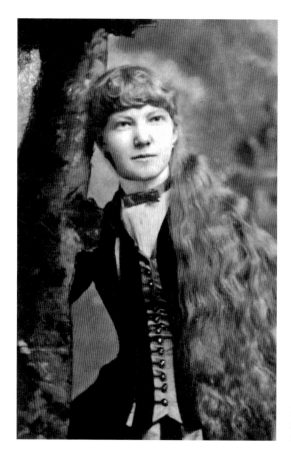

Nelle Nance at sixteen. *Courtesy of the Rhodes College Archives and Special Collections, Memphis, Tennessee.*

thought of in the Brownsville community, as indicated in the article about their wedding:

> *Miss Nance has lived here for several years, having charge of the musical department of the Brownsville Female College, and is loved and esteemed by all. Mr. Halliburton, upon whom Dame Fortune has showered with so many blessings, is one of Haywood County's most prominent and prosperous young farmers and capitalists. Many prominent people from this and adjoining states were present.*[9]

After their marriage, they boarded in the home of Richard and Mary McLemore Thomas at 719 Key Corner in Brownsville. Originally, the red brick house had been a log cabin built around 1870 by Mary's father, Sugars McLemore, one of Brownsville's original settlers. Mary Thomas and her husband copied the style of a house they liked in St. Louis and remodeled the log cabin into one of Brownsville's most stylish homes at the time. It was in this historic house that Richard Halliburton was born on January 9, 1900. Richard and Nelle Halliburton searched for a name for their firstborn, finally settling on "Richard" to honor the first settler of Brownsville, Colonel Richard Nixon. Years later, Richard Halliburton humorously prefaced a story in his book *New Worlds to Conquer* with a mention of his Brownsville namesake. He wrote, "I was called Richard after the town's patriarch whose life had been so distinguished for wisdom and prudence…it was hoped that I in receiving his name might also receive his virtues. Considering the story I am about to relate, it is clear that this hope was not fulfilled."[10]

Shortly after Halliburton was born, the family moved to 207 North Garland in Memphis, Tennessee, and Wesley Halliburton began working in the farm real estate and timber business. On May 31, 1902, Wesley Jr. was born, and the young family thrived both socially and economically. Halliburton's business was doing very well, and he quickly made many important business connections in Memphis. The family had a housekeeper, were members of civic clubs and could afford to take time off from work for long vacations and trips abroad. Although Memphis was a growing urban community around the turn of the century, its female residents were expected to stay home and stay quiet. It would be twenty more years before Tennessee became the thirty-sixth state to ratify the Nineteenth Amendment, clearing the way for its official adoption eight days later, thus allowing Nelle Halliburton and other women to vote. Memphis journalist Robert Talley described the period shortly before the Halliburtons arrived in Memphis from Brownsville. He wrote, "Bewhiskered 'Pappy' Hadden was Mayor of the little city of Memphis and toured the cobblestoned streets in a buggy drawn by Hulda his white mule…'Fiddlin' Bob Taylor was Governor of Tennessee…Benjamin Harrison was President of the United States…and, quite definitely in the opinion of most people, [the] woman's place was in the home."[11]

Memphis may have been a traditional town, but Nelle Halliburton would never be a traditional turn-of-the-century housewife—and all indications are that her many interests and activities outside the home were appreciated and encouraged by her husband.

Their youngest son, Wesley Halliburton Jr., excelled at sports and became an active, popular little boy, while his older brother Richard preferred to spend time writing, drawing or riding Roxy, the family's pony. Years later, when introducing Richard Halliburton at an event in Memphis, his father

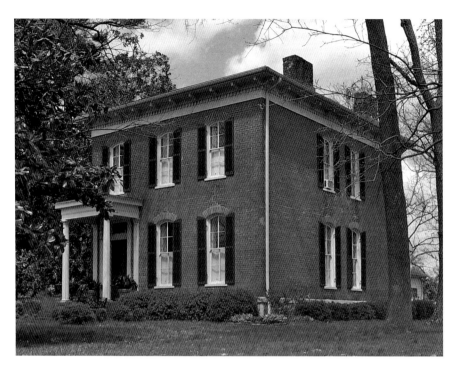

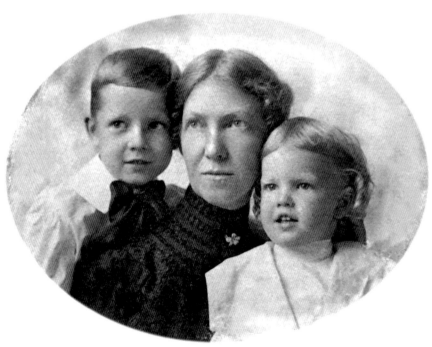

reminisced, "While he was a virile boy, he never quite entered the billy-goat period of boyhood nor cared to become one of the gang. Fire engines and locomotives did not excite him very much, and a fat policeman was not his idea of a hero; he rather leaned towards Odysseus and King Arthur and Marco Polo…and his father."[12]

Halliburton's earliest schooling began at home from his mother's friend Mary Hutchison, and later he and Wesley Jr. were both sent to Memphis University School, which was attended by boys from some of the most well-connected families in Memphis. The hot, humid summers of West Tennessee were spent golfing with friends, visiting family back home in Brownsville or fishing at the family cabin in Tate Springs, Arkansas.

For the Halliburtons, the turn of the century had brought happiness, success and prosperity. Nothing could have prepared them for both the thrilling triumphs and heartbreaking tragedies that were right around the corner.

Opposite, top: The Brownsville, Tennessee house where Richard Halliburton was born on January 9, 1900. *Author's collection.*

Opposite, bottom: Richard, Nelle and Wesley Halliburton Jr. *Courtesy of the Rhodes College Archives and Special Collections, Memphis, Tennessee.*

CHAPTER 2

Mary Hutchison

May 20, 2012

Hutchison's commencement exercises on Monday will mark a transcendent day in the school's 110-year history. A century ago in May of 1912, Mary Grimes Hutchison held her school's first formal commencement exercises with five students that she had begun teaching 10 years earlier. The school was housed in the old Nineteenth Century Club at Poplar and Third. On Monday, 56 girls will follow the 100-year tradition of becoming Hutchison graduates.
—Commercial Appeal

The fifth member of the Halliburton family, Mary Grimes Hutchison, made a big impact on young Richard Halliburton, and the two remained close throughout his life. Born to Nathan and Mary Hutchison in Kansas City, Missouri, on September 29, 1872, Hutchison's childhood, like that of Wesley and Nelle Halliburton, would also be filled with loss. By the time she was fourteen, she had lost both parents and the grandmother who raised her. As a child, she knew she wanted to be a teacher, and at some point very early in her life, she decided that she would never marry. At sixteen, she wrote, "In a graystone house all covered with vines, I'll dwell as a mistress with never a lord. He wishes to order, my will to tame, for what my name is right today, in the far off future, t'will be the same."[13]

Relatives sent the shy, quiet orphan to Science Hill School in Shelbyville, Kentucky, which was one of the oldest and most respected girls' preparatory schools in the South at the time. After graduating, she began fulfilling her dream of being a teacher by accepting a position at the Athens (Tennessee) Female College. It was there that she met the outgoing music teacher, Nelle Nance, and the two opposites became immediate friends. After Hutchison left Athens for another teaching position back in Kentucky and Nance began her job at the Brownsville Female College, Nance missed her friend so much that she helped secure a position for her at the college in Brownsville. After Nance married Wesley Halliburton and moved to Memphis, Hutchison continued her teaching career for several years in Brownsville. Her reputation as a great teacher was quickly established. One of her especially strong students, Robert Thomas, had gone from her school in Brownsville to West Point Military Academy. It was said the influence of his hometown education was obvious and was attributed to Hutchison. In 1902, around the time Wesley Jr. was born, Nelle Halliburton and several of her neighbors convinced Hutchison to move to Memphis to teach their young children. She initially lived with the Halliburton family, and her first Memphis classes were held in their home. Eventually, she began teaching only young women and ran her classes out of several small houses in Memphis. Students were added quickly as her reputation spread and her school outgrew numerous buildings. From a house on the corner of Union and Cleveland to the Nineteenth Century Club at Poplar and Third, where her friend Nelle Halliburton was an active member, she finally settled for a while at 1129 Union Avenue. Referred to by Memphians at the time as the "Old Love Place," this would be the building she would refer to as "her first real school." An ad for the school that appeared around this time read:

Miss Hutchison's School
A Well-Equipped College Preparatory School
French taught in all grades by natural method.
Advantages in music, domestic art, physical training and expression.
Convenient to three car lines.
Cum. Tel. 1496 Hemlock[14]

Another of her young students during those early years, Marguerite Randolph Turner, later remembered Hutchison as being "gentle but firm, sympathetic and kind, a tolerant, soft-spoken disciplinarian, very tall, very thin, and very proper. She dressed severely with high collars on her long neck. She had great big brown eyes and wore her hair in a bun on top of her head."[15]

Hutchison remained close to her friends Wesley and Nelle Halliburton, and because the two young Halliburton boys had no living grandparents,

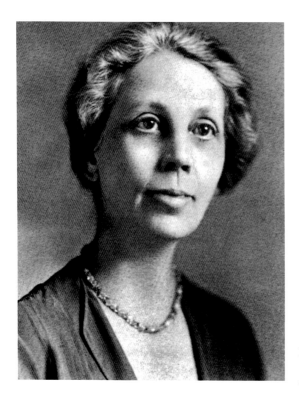

Mary Grimes Hutchison in 1929. *Courtesy of Hutchison School, Memphis, Tennessee.*

Hutchison saw a role for herself in the family and became the children's designated grandmother. Although the adult Halliburtons both referred to their friend as "Hutchie," very early, they encouraged their son to call her "grandmother." As a toddler, Richard Halliburton's pronuncation of "grandmother" was "Ammudder," and that became the name he used for her throughout his life. Letters young Halliburton wrote to Hutchison when he was a boy illustrate just how close they were. When he was twelve, he wrote, "If only you knew how bad I want to see you! And just to think, I won't see you for another six weeks. I will write you often and you, of course, will write to me and that will patch things up."[16] The lessons Hutchison taught Richard and their close friendship would influence him greatly, especially as he began to deal with a sudden, unexplained illness.

CHAPTER 3

Heartsick

July 7, 1940
Richard was a dutiful son. Although he shipped to Europe as a deck hand on a lumber boat without his parents' consent before he had finished Princeton, he never failed to write letters to his father and mother at home. He was tender in his regard for them…and they were continually anxious about him. So wherever he might be, in whatever far corner of the globe, he thought of them.
—Kansas City Star

In January 1915, just before he turned fifteen, Richard Halliburton began to complain of symptoms that were diagnosed as tachycardia or "a rapidly beating heart." While a rapid heartbeat can be caused by anxiety or fever, it can also be a sign of a more serious illness like lung disease, pneumonia or thyroid problems. The Halliburtons and Mary Hutchison had all experienced the pain and grief of having family members die young, and all three adults doted on Halliburton and his younger brother, so it's easy to imagine the panic an "illness of the heart" would trigger in their young family. Richard was taken out of school and prescribed bed rest by the family doctor. The disease is not life threatening, and today many cases of tachycardia require no treatment, as the "racing heartbeat" children complain of usually goes away on its own. After four months of bed rest, however, Halliburton's health was still not showing any signs of improvement, so the family began looking outside Memphis for solutions.

If you had the means in 1915, the Battle Creek Sanitarium in Battle Creek, Michigan, was the perfect place to go if you were suffering from a variety of

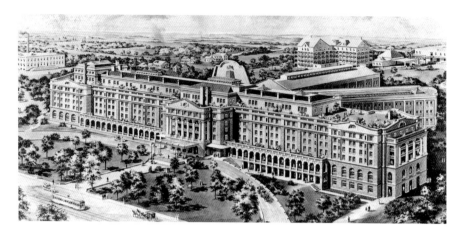

The Battle Creek Sanitarium in Battle Creek, Michigan. *Author's collection.*

ailments. The hospital was operated by the Seventh Day Adventist Church, and rather than treat just an illness, the philosophy of the resort's eccentric chief medical operator, John Harvey Kellogg, was to treat the whole person by fostering social and psychological health in addition to physical health. Kellogg and his medical team also placed a great deal of emphasis on nutrition, enemas and exercise. This was the same Kellogg who, along with his brother, was the inventor of Kellogg's corn flakes. Perhaps before the Halliburtons left for Battle Creek, their family doctor showed them an ad for the "San" that could be seen in magazines around the time Halliburton was ill. If he did, it probably made Wesley Halliburton, with his practical nature, question whether a stay at the San would really offer a cure for his young son. The ad stated:

> *Brain fog—mental confusion—indecision—lack of vim and chronic weariness are evidence of something wrong with the body. To determine the causes of ill health by a complete scientific "inventory" of each patient's entire organism is an essential feature of the Battle Creek Sanitarium System.*
>
> *In addition to the usual physical examination, the efficiency of the whole body is measured; chemists and bacteriologists examine the bodily excretions, the blood and stomach contents; physical trainers test the physique and the muscles; other specialists study the heart, lungs, stomach and other vital internal organs.*
>
> *Then follows a course of health training adapted to each patient's special needs—diet scientifically regulated, graduated body-building exercises,*

> *outdoor methods, the scientific application of the electric light, hydrotherapy, electricity, mechanical and electrical exercises, radium, the E-ray, massage and all other up-to-date remedial means.*[17]

Another ad that appeared in magazines around the same time promised, "Even the air inspires new health." In addition to the air, the ad pointed out the importance of exercise at the San. "There are pleasant walks, with trainers or attendants. For those so inclined, there are sleighing, skeeing [*sic*], tobogganing, skating and walking parties—outdoor and indoor amusements." The health resort had already been in place for nearly fifty years when the Halliburtons decided that a stay at the San could possibly cure their fifteen-year-old son's heart problems. There were not many young patients at the San. According to the facility's annual report, in 1915 it treated 5,495 patients, with twenty-nine days being the average stay for men and boys. Only 132 of those patients were children aged fifteen or younger, like Halliburton.[18]

Catering primarily to the wealthy, the San was also a place to see and be seen, and you were likely to meet important people and celebrities of the day on the golf course or while strolling along the rooftop veranda. The list of the resort's notable patients through the years is long and diverse and includes actors Johnny Weissmuller and Sarah Bernhard; wife of Abraham Lincoln, Mary Todd Lincoln; founder of the Ford Motor Company, Henry Ford; the twenty-ninth president of the United States, Warren G. Harding; and famed abolitionist Sojourner Truth. According to the annual report for 1915, the patients' occupations for the year of Halliburton's stay included two advertisers, one actor, 156 attorneys, 108 bankers, three chauffeurs, one congressman, seven editors, two ex-governors, forty-three insurance agents and nearly two thousand housewives.

Halliburton's stay exposed him to the value of physical activity and exercise, which he would embrace for the rest of his life. From swimming and skiing to walking and climbing, his eventual career as an adventure and travel writer would require him to draw from the skills to which he was exposed that summer.

Another benefit of his months at the San, and something that would greatly impact the trajectory of his life and ultimate career, was the introduction of Halliburton to boys who attended a private school called Lawrenceville. Halliburton quickly developed a clear vision for his future. In a letter to his father written from the San, he wrote, "The L. boys love their school. I will be near New York surrounded by friends. I have my heart set on Princeton—50

The Battle Creek Sanitarium

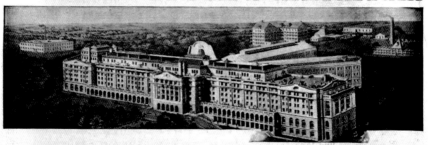

Here, The Very Air Inspires New Health

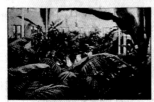

The Palm Garden

INSIDE the Battle Creek Sanitarium you will find a perfect "Florida Climate"—hygienically maintained—never *hot*, just *warm*, with perfect ventilation. Bananas ripen in the great garden-of-palms—and other tropical plants. And our sun parlors, rest foyers, and our cozy nooks tempt one to rest for mind and body.

Outside is the famous Michigan winter air—clear, pure; full of tingles and fine inspiration.

There are pleasant walks, with trainers or attendants. For those so inclined, there are sleighing, skeeing, tobogganing, skating and walking parties—outdoor and indoor amusements.

Time never hangs heavily here—not even an invalid's time.

When a patient comes, the first thing is a thorough and scientific examination of his case. Then, a special day's program is marked out for him—something interesting and helpful to do every hour of the day.

The Battle Creek Sanitarium system seeks to cure by correcting wrong habits of life and rebuilding the body. Results usually begin to appear quickly.

The baths prescribed comprise 200 or more kinds, including Nauheim, and Electric Light, Electricity, Finsen Ray, Massage, Mechanical Vibration, Manual Swedish Movements; indoor swimming pools; the great gymnasium, with class and individual instructors; trained nurses; expert bath attendants, both men and women. Accommodations and service first-class—equal to those of the best hotels.

Rates Are Reasonable

The outlay for room, board, baths, bath attendants and necessary medical attention, is no more than is charged for room and board alone at any first-class winter resort hotel.

Our beautiful book of photographic views gives glimpses of the Great Battle Creek Sanitarium buildings, and illustrates the methods and advantages of the Battle Creek Sanitarium System.

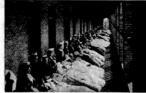

One of the Outing Porches

Kindly send coupon, and address Box 122.

The Sanitarium, Battle Creek, Mich.

THE SANITARIUM
Box 122, Battle Creek, Mich.

Without obligating me in any way, I will be pleased to receive the Book of Views mentioned in this advertisement.

Name ....
Address ....
City ....
State ....

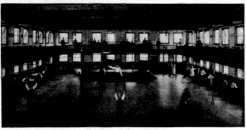

Section of Gymnasium

When you write please mention HAMPTON'S MAGAZINE

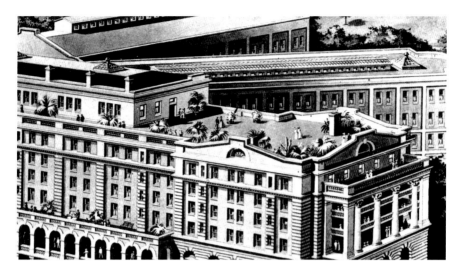

One of the rooftop terraces at the Battle Creek Sanitarium in Battle Creek, Michigan. *Author's collection*.

Opposite: Ad for the Battle Creek Sanitarium in *Hampton's* magazine. *Author's collection*.

L. boys go into Princeton every year."[19] Halliburton did go to Lawrenceville, and after he graduated and moved on to Princeton in 1918, his younger brother followed in his footsteps and became a Lawrenceville student himself.

Wesley Halliburton Jr. was strong, athletic and popular. No doubt Richard was proud to introduce his good-looking younger brother "Wes," as the family called him, to his friends and fellow students still at Lawrenceville, and Wes was grateful to have his popular older brother close by as he began a new school so far away from home. Princeton was only six miles from Lawrenceville, so the boys were able to spend time together.

In November, Wes Halliburton wasn't feeling well. Within a few short weeks, what had begun as a sore throat and cough became chest pains, difficulty breathing and a fever that wouldn't go away. Both boys were disappointed when the younger brother had to return home to Memphis to recuperate. But since the semester was nearly over anyway, they likely thought he would simply return and continue his studies in a few weeks. Halliburton returned home to Memphis for the Christmas holidays and was able to spend time with his brother, whose health had still not improved. In fact, it was getting much worse.

On January 1, 1918, while the rest of the city of Memphis was slowly waking up and shaking off the after effects of New Year's Eve parties and

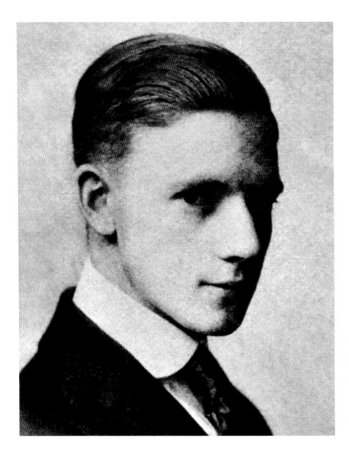

Richard Halliburton in 1916, shortly after leaving the Battle Creek Sanitarium. *Courtesy of the Rhodes College Archives and Special Collections, Memphis, Tennessee.*

fireworks over the Mississippi River, the Halliburton family was grieving the death of their youngest member. At the house that morning, the doctor wrote the following words on Wes's death certificate: "acute rheumatic endocarditis brought on by acute rheumatic pericarditis."[20] In other words, Wes Halliburton died from rheumatic fever. A strep infection he possibly caught in his early days at Lawrenceville had damaged the valves of his heart beyond repair. Many years later, their father shared his memories of that night with his friend James Cortese, who wrote:

> *One night as we sat up talking in his study, the father told me about the death of his younger son: "I was sitting, holding him on my lap—it seemed the only way he could get comfortable, sitting up. And as we sat there, he died. I called to Nelle and Richard, 'Wesley's gone!'" The weary old eyes closed and we sat in silence, he with his memories, I in sympathy.*[21]

Halliburton's niece Juliet Halliburton Davis was at the Halliburton home afterward and remembered a minister trying to offer condolences by stating it was "God's will." Understandably, the grieving father asked angrily, "What kind of God would take the life of such a fine young boy?"[22]

Certainly, the irony of Wes Halliburton's death was not lost on his older brother. For years, Richard Halliburton had been the sick one, while his younger brother was the athletic, healthy one in the family. Richard had been warned to stay calm and not to exert himself for fear that his heart problems would return. Now, it was the young, vibrant brother whose heart had failed. Several years later, on the occasion of what would have been his younger brother's birthday, Richard wrote their mother, "Year by year we drift farther away from the time when he was such a vital part of our family, when it was impossible to contemplate the four of us being ever any more or any less, but the succeeding years can never dim the memory of him as he was when he was fifteen. He will still be so when we are old. He would have been nineteen today, almost grown…we can always remember him as a fine-looking curly-haired youth."[23]

CHAPTER 4

Memphis to New Orleans and Beyond

October 13, 1935
Richard's worst escapade, or so it seemed at the time to his distracted parents, was when he ran away from home at 19. He was to spend the week with relatives at Brownsville, Tenn., while his parents attended a house party in Mississippi.
—Commercial Appeal

On July 14, 1919, Richard Halliburton ran away from home. Perhaps a better description was that he was running away from the sort of life he knew his parents were anticipating for him and toward the romance and excitement of the unknown. He had experienced his younger brother's untimely death, and it was eating away at him. In a letter Halliburton sent his parents later, he explained leaving was the only way to end his "restless, useless, unhappy existence."[24]

After returning to Princeton, Halliburton had convinced himself that if he could make it until the next summer, he could then begin the life of adventure he so desperately desired. He later shared with his parents that he had been so depressed and restless those months after Wes's death that he would find himself in tears for no reason.[25]

The day Richard ran away to Europe, Nelle Halliburton pulled up at Memphis's Union Station and dropped off a very nervous but excited young man. He must have seemed anxious to her, but she thought he was only taking a short train ride to Brownsville for a visit with family friends Atha and Woodleif Thomas. Two years older than Halliburton, the twins were the sons

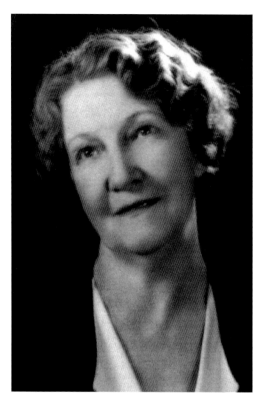

A professional portrait of Nelle Halliburton. *Courtesy of the Rhodes College Archives and Special Collections, Memphis, Tennessee.*

of Spencer and Kate Fanning Thomas, and Halliburton had spent a great deal of time with the family as a boy. Their father was one of the organizers of the Brownsville Bank and held a variety of civic positions in city government there. When talking about that day years later, Nelle Halliburton would remember she thought it strange her son stood on the platform and waved goodbye until she had driven completely down the street and out of sight. What she didn't know until later was that Halliburton was holding back tears, which he said came the moment she was gone.[26]

Rather than board the next train for Brownsville, Richard had been planning for some time to board the 12:05 Meridian & Memphis headed south to New Orleans. The next day, Nelle and Wesley Halliburton were planning to leave for a short trip out of town to visit with friends. In Richard's plan, his parents would leave Memphis early the next morning and never even become aware that he had not gone to Brownsville. The following Tuesday, his father would arrive at his office and find a letter Richard had mailed from New Orleans, and all would be well. The only flaw in his scheme was in not making Atha Thomas aware of the plan. Everything fell apart the following day when Thomas showed up in Memphis looking for Richard.

Mother, father and son would later all have slightly different memories of what happened next. Richard related to a friend that his parents "went wild" and claimed an article was placed in the local paper that included the words "foul play feared." His father, while downplaying his own worries to Richard's mother, quietly phoned hotels in the area to see if their son might have checked in "with a girl." His mother would remember "four days of frantic search." Of course, his family and friends were greatly relieved when, as his father had predicted, the postman brought a letter from Richard Halliburton to his office that Tuesday morning.

The elder Halliburton, possibly just relieved that his son was alive, first sent a telegram of encouragement:

> *7/19/19*
> *Richard Halliburton*
> *Cosmopolitan Hotel*
> *Go to it and may you have a bully time. A little surprised yes. Don't fail to write us. For God's sake take care of yourself, but get this out of your system. Wishing you bon voyage. Dad.*

He followed it up with a letter chastising his son for causing his mother so much worry. But Richard certainly meant no intentional harm to his mother. It could be argued that he had the freedom to travel and explore and live the life of an adventurer because his mother and father offered him a consistent source of love and stability back in Memphis, which he appreciated. Throughout his life, Richard wrote more than one thousand lengthy letters to his parents on topics ranging from what he had for dinner and who he saw at what party to the successes and struggles he encountered during his career. However, like everyone, his letters were written with the recipients in mind, and he wrote to his parents only what he wanted them to know. In 1942, Richard's father released a book of his son's letters called *Richard Halliburton: His Stories of His Life's Adventures*. A Halliburton researcher, Chip Deffaa, later determined that the elder Halliburton had edited the letters, removing content that did not present his son the way he wanted.[27]

One letter in particular, written a few months after he had departed for Europe, offered an exchange between father and son that summarized well the different life philosophies of each. Richard wrote from Paris on December 5, 1919, in response to his father's statement that he wished his son was "at Princeton living in the tenor of your way." His answer leaves little doubt as to his state of mind and offers a glimpse at the philosophy he would embrace throughout his life:

> *I hate that expression and as far as I am able I intend to avoid that condition. When impulse and spontaneity fail to make my "way" as uneven as possible, then I shall sit up nights inventing means of making life as*

conglomerate and vivid as possible. Those who live in the even tenor of their way simply exist until death ends their monotonous tranquility. No, there's going to be no even tenor with me.[28]

About the time the family realized their only son had not gone to Brownsville and was now missing, Richard was waking up at the Cosmopolitan Hotel and beginning what would be several weeks of exploration of the city of New Orleans. While there, he would spend time exploring the French market and Jackson Square, visiting the historic Cabildo and going swimming in Lake Pontchartrain. Although he was quickly hired as the lowest rank of merchant seaman on the *Octorara*, he had arrived during a seamen's strike, and it would be three weeks before the ship finally set sail. Halliburton wrote about those initial days at sea, which caused him to be "sick in body and terrified in mind." He later told the story that when the ship docked at Hampton Roads in Virginia, he took the opportunity to ask the captain for a leave so he could go visit his parents, who were also in Virginia at the time. As Halliburton told the story, he let his mother know he had no intention of going back to the ship, but she forced him to return, instilling in him the belief that "if I surrendered this time to adversity I would lose all respect for myself and never again have the courage to take charge of my own destiny." Although very likely fabricated, this story had great appeal for the mothers with whom he would share it at ladies club meetings and lunches through the years.

When the ship pulled into port in Hull, England, in mid-September, Halliburton's first opportunity to explore another country on his own was underway. The letters he wrote and sent home to his family in Memphis and to his friends back at Princeton offered the first glimpse of what would ultimately make him one of the most famous writers of his day. His curiosity and need for adventure would inspire him to do something unique, and then his desire to share it with others would drive him to write about it. He recorded many adventures during his early travels, and while the basic facts are mostly all true, he admittedly embellished some of his stories to make them more interesting and exciting to the reader—whether that be his parents, his friends or, years later, the fans of his books, articles and personal appearances.

On his first night in Europe, Halliburton did a most American thing—he went to a Charlie Chaplin movie. In a letter home, he shared the experience in a style that would become his trademark. Rather than just stating the fact that he went to a movie, he wrote of an adventure that took place in the setting of the movie theater, with himself as the central character and fun-loving hero:

> *I passed a side entrance to the theater on my way to the front and found a bunch of gamins four to eight years old bubbling with excitement over seeing Charlie. I took about half a dozen in with me for a shilling or so and they were delighted beyond measure. One of the four-year-olds insisted on sitting on his benefactor's lap so I could read him the leaders. Charlie in* Sunnyside *was not half so amusing to me as the kids who almost fell out of their seats.*[29]

Did Richard Halliburton really take six street urchins into a Charlie Chaplin movie on his first night in England? Possibly. But the possibility also exists that he went to a Charlie Chaplin movie and, when entering, saw a group of children on the street and thought to himself, "Wouldn't it be interesting if I…" As he explained in later years, he simply took the truth and then "splashed a little red paint in it."

His eight months in Europe were filled with adventures in London, Paris, Marseilles, Monte Carlo and the Riviera. He toured St. Paul's Cathedral, experienced his first flight in an airplane, slept in a three-hundred-year-old inn, walked to Versailles, toured the birthplace of Shakespeare and spent Christmas 1919 in the South of France.

Halliburton set sail for home in mid-January 1920 on the French liner *La Savoie*, which he called "the bummest boat still afloat," drawing to a close the first of a lifetime of adventures to be brought on by his "uneasy tenor."

CHAPTER 5

Higher Education

January 17, 1930
The much-publicized Richard Halliburton '21, author, adventurer, lecturer, canal swimmer, etc., when interviewed by the Princetonian, *said, among other things, "One must have the creature urge. He has to love and like to do it." And, surprisingly enough, he was speaking of writing at the time.*
—Princetonian Alumni Weekly

After leaving the Battle Creek Sanitarium, Richard Halliburton decided to attend the Lawrenceville School in Lawrenceville, New Jersey, specifically because it was a feeder school for Princeton University. His father would have preferred that he stay closer to home, but both parents had benefited greatly from boarding schools, so his protests were likely weak. Lawrenceville was initially founded by Isaac Brown in 1810 and was originally called Maidenhead Academy. By the time Halliburton was moving his trunks into one of the campus "houses," the school was widely known and respected around the country. It sat on more than seven hundred acres, and Frederick Law Olmsted, famous for his design of Central Park in New York City, also created the park-like campus for Lawrenceville. Proud of its Presbyterian heritage and a student body from the "right" kind of families, each year the school attracted four hundred more boys largely of "the second generation" (boys whose parents were born in the United States) from all over the country.[30] Around that time, 40 percent of the students attended Princeton after graduation. Lawrenceville was a school with a very distinct culture and introduced some concepts from English schools into the American college prep school system. For example, Lawrenceville was one of the first schools where boys lived together in houses on campus. They were essentially small communities of students, each with a headmaster who "nurtured the boy's intellectual development and personal growth."[31] Owen Johnson, an alumnus of Lawrenceville, used memories of life at the school to write his 1910 novel, *The Varmint*, which was about the adventures of a young student, Dink Stover, and his experiences at the school. The book was such a success that Johnson wrote more stories, which were published in the *Saturday Evening Post*, and the series became known as *The Lawrenceville Stories*. In 1950, Metro-Goldwyn-Mayer released *The Happy Years*, a Hollywood version of *The Varmint* starring Dean Stockwell. Much of the movie was filmed on the Lawrenceville School campus and shows off Olmstead's gardens and many of the Queen Anne–style buildings. The 1907 version of *The Lawrenceville School Register*, a guide produced for parents of potential students, explains the type of boys the school was seeking:

> *The standard of scholarship and methods of instruction are of such a character that boys who have not average aptitude for acquiring knowledge and a reasonable willingness to study should not seek admission to the institution. Boys with a record of failure in other schools are not likely to succeed here.*
>
> *Applicants for admission to the First Form should be at least twelve years of age, and must give evidence, by written testimonials from former teachers and by examination, of good attainments in spelling, reading, writing, geography, English grammar, and elementary arithmetic at least through percentage.*

Halliburton entered Lawrenceville in the fall of 1916 and quickly became editor-in-chief of the school newspaper, the *Lawrence*. He thrived at the exclusive prep school and met a group of friends with whom he would remain close throughout his life. Included in the group were Irvine O. "Mike" Hockaday, Edward L. "Larry" Keyes III, John Henry "Heinie" Leh, James Penfield "Shorty" Seiberling and Channing "Chan" Sweet. Halliburton's talent for writing and his creativity were noticed at the school, and he was selected to write the words and music for the song the class of 1917 performed on graduation day. The country was experiencing the First World War, and the threat of having to go to battle certainly impacted the young students' lives. American patriotism

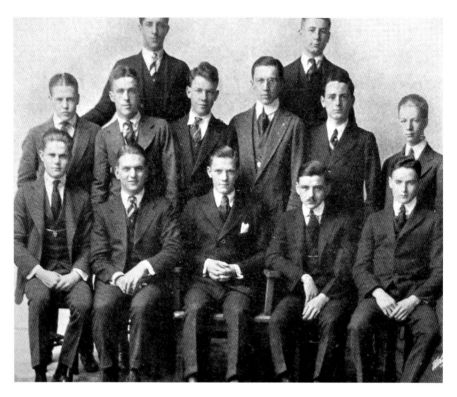

The board of the *Lawrence*, a newspaper produced by students at the Lawrenceville School. Richard Halliburton is front row, center. *Courtesy of the Rhodes College Archives and Special Collections, Memphis, Tennessee.*

was at an all-time high and can be detected in the second chorus of the ode Halliburton wrote:

> *Restraining gates are opened wide,*
> *Ten thousand paths lead from this door,*
> *God made us men to face the world,*
> *Whatever lies before.*
> *If we fight we must beyond the sea,*
> *Trust us till we come back to thee;*
> *America, America,*
> *Trust us till we come back to thee.*

Halliburton's own words, written four years later as he was preparing to graduate from Princeton, best show the fondness he had for Lawrenceville:

Feeling very rested, I could not resist the outdoors—I put on my walking shoes and followed the canal back through the woods and fields to the road leading to L'ville (all alone) and struck across to the old school coming down upon it in the twilight from above. They, too, were having a vacation, and no lights were on. Never has it seemed so appealing. A rush of emotions and memories came over me as I looked from Kennedy House to Upper and the other familiar haunts of the benign spot.[32]

Halliburton and his friends from Lawrenceville entered Princeton University in the fall of 1917. By the time they graduated four years later, they had experienced a war, a brief postwar depression and the beginnings of the affluent decade that would come to be known as both the "Roaring Twenties" and the "Jazz Age."

Originally a school for Presbyterian ministers, Princeton University was founded in Elizabeth, New Jersey, in 1746 as the College of New Jersey. It wasn't until 1896 that its name was changed to Princeton. During the sesquicentennial celebration of that year, class of 1879 alumni and future president of the United States Woodrow Wilson delivered the keynote address, *Princeton in the Nation's Service*. This would become the school's mantra and has been associated with the university ever since. Wilson would go on to be elected president of Princeton in 1902 and serve until 1910.

When he took on the duties of president, Wilson was well aware that the academic side of the college experience at the school ranked a distant third behind club life and campus social activities. Wilson's predecessor, Francis Landly Patton, was a Presbyterian theologian noted for his casual administrative style and his dislike of disciplinary and academic standards. At one faculty meeting, he reportedly announced, "Gentlemen, whether we like it or not, we shall have to recognize that Princeton is a rich man's college, and rich men do not frequently come to college to study."[33] One faculty member remembered Patton stating, "I have no belief in discipline and it's good for a young man to come to college, even if he did no more than rub his shoulders against the buildings."[34] The culture and attitudes of the Princeton that Halliburton and his Lawrenceville friends entered was later immortalized in *This Side of Paradise*, the classic novel written by F. Scott Fitzgerald, who also attended Princeton. Fitzgerald referred to the college as "the pleasantest country club in America" and, in an essay written for *College Humor*, noted that Princeton was out of place in New Jersey, referring to it as "a green Phoenix rising out of the ugliest country

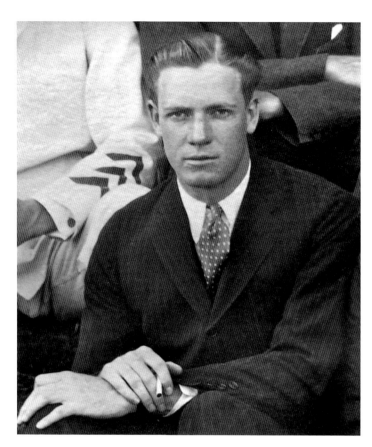

Richard Halliburton at Princeton University. *Courtesy of the Rhodes College Archives and Special Collections, Memphis, Tennessee.*

in the world."[35] Ironically, the protagonist of Fitzgerald's *Paradise* novel is a handsome Princeton University student who struggles with greed and seeks to reach a higher status—certainly accusations Halliburton would have to deal with at the university and, later, in his own writing career. Although the value placed on academics had grown considerably under Wilson's administration, Princeton was still a place where clubs, sports and social activities could take precedence over studies. Many wealthy parents sent their sons off to Ivy League universities for the connections they would make rather than for the education they would receive.

The summer after Halliburton entered Princeton, a training camp was opened, and every young man was required to train with a branch of the armed forces. Halliburton selected the navy to increase his chances to possibly travel overseas. The war officially ended on November 11, 1918, with the Treaty of Versailles, and Halliburton and his peers were free to return their focus to their studies, sports and social lives. Halliburton was also now free to focus on his writing. When the *Daily Princetonian* was seeking an additional member for its board, he was one of eight young men who applied. Each had to provide news samples, which were then evaluated based on "quantity, quality and fitness of the news." Halliburton was selected for the position.

The letters to his mother and father during this time are filled with many details regarding schoolwork, teachers and friends, along with other details most boys away from home for college never think of sharing with their parents. In one letter, he noted that the "club elections" were coming soon and that he was going to make sure he and his friends got into the best one. The elections were for the eating clubs of Princeton, which were similar to modern-day fraternities and sororities. The first students at the university had eaten their meals in local boardinghouses, and these students formed clubs based on where they were eating. Each club had a tendency to dissolve once the students graduated and moved on. In 1879, a group of ambitious students rented a building and created an eating club that would continue from year to year. The endeavor was such a success that four years later, they built a house on Prospect Avenue specifically for the eating club. By 1900, most juniors and seniors were eating in clubs along the same street, and the popularity of this practice continued to grow despite frustration among some students and faculty over who got into which club. Halliburton wrote to his father on March 10, 1919:

> *The club elections come soon. For some reason I've taken the responsibility of my crowd onto my shoulders. I'm going to get us into the best club on Prospect Street or bust. I'm just bursting with schemes—and I'm sorry because I worry over it. Sometimes I ardently wish I were one of the phlegmatic kind of students that stick to their books regularly and don't strain over anything and are too insensitive to worry over lack of position or influence. Often they leave college with a better mental capacity to handle life and business.*[36]

In another letter, written six weeks later, he shared the outcome with his parents. His group of sixteen friends had been told that only some would be accepted into the Cap and Gown eating club. As a group, they stayed unified in protest, and all sixteen were eventually admitted in the club. F. Scott Fitzgerald described this particular club in *This Side of Paradise* as being "anti-alcoholic, faintly religious and politically powerful."

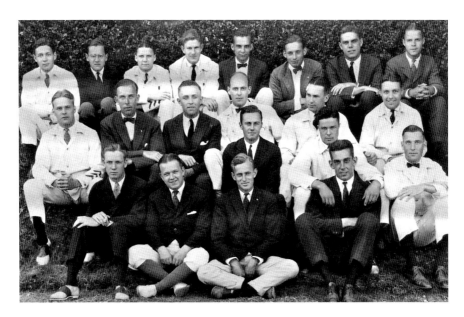

Richard Halliburton (front row, left) and the class of 1921 at Princeton University. *Courtesy of the Rhodes College Archives and Special Collections, Memphis, Tennessee.*

Of course, parents who had lost a child would be anxious with their only remaining son so far away, and the Halliburtons' concern for Richard's health can be detected in one of his letters back to them assuring his parents that he was "obeying your orders about running." One letter includes references that would have been especially meaningful for a father who came from the cotton fields of Haywood County, Tennessee. Halliburton wrote, "I am as healthy as a bunch of Johnson grass in a cotton field, and no doubt cause as much trouble to my cultivators."[37]

Halliburton's vagabond escape to Europe impressed his Princeton classmates, and although after his adventure he returned to Princeton midway through the next term, he was voted most original member of his class and was elected editor-in-chief of the *Princeton Pictorial*. The summer of 1920 gave Halliburton the sort of validation his father, too, would appreciate when he sold his first article as a travel writer. He and three classmates went on a backpacking trip in the Rocky Mountains, and from that experience, Halliburton wrote an article he was able to sell to *Field & Stream* for $150.

CHAPTER 6

Post Princeton

June 10, 1932
Still traveling the "Royal Road to Romance," but now choosing the airplane as his transport vehicle, Richard Halliburton, young globe-trotting author, stopped in Akron Thursday to visit his old friend and schoolmate, J. Penfield Seiberling, 425 N. Portage Path. The pair attended the Lawrenceville, N.J. preparatory school together 17 years ago and were roommates at Princeton.
—Akron (OH) Journal

Three events took place in Richard Halliburton's life in the year before he graduated that helped shape his post-Princeton plans: an Easter holiday at Harpers Ferry with his father, a dinner with famed travel writer Harry Franck and the great success of the *Pic*, the Princeton magazine for which he was editor-in-chief.

First, Halliburton needed to let his father know he had no intentions of following in his businessman footsteps. Wesley Halliburton hoped that when his son graduated, he would join him in the family business, find a Memphis socialite to marry and produce many little Halliburtons for he and his wife to spoil. Richard Halliburton knew the life for which his Princeton roommates were all headed was exactly what his father expected, but it was absolutely nothing like what he intended for himself. In the first pages of his book *The Royal Road to Romance*, Halliburton described an evening in the boy's dorm room as they were preparing for exams. John Leh frowned into an accounting book, James Seiberling was yawning over an essay on corporate finance, Larry Keyes was absorbed in protoplasm and Irvine Hockaday was struggling to keep his mind on constitutional government. As much as Halliburton loved his friends, he wrote, "They were so restrained, so infallible, so super-sane, so utterly indifferent to the divine madness of the spring moonlight." He thought of himself as the exact opposite of what he felt they were. He continued, "I glanced at the heavy textbook in my hand, and swore at the man who wrote it. Economics!—how could one be expected to moil over such dullness when the perfume and the moon and all the demoralizing lure of a May evening were seething one's brain?"[38]

As their college years were coming to an end, and all five boys were looking ahead to what would come next, Halliburton must have felt more disconnected and different from his friends than he had ever felt before. Although he knew he was not like them in many ways, their normalcy seemed to propel him toward the sort of life he imagined. In fact, he dedicated *The Royal Road to Romance* to his four friends with the inscription "whose sanity, consistency and respectability as Princeton roommates drove me to this book."

Not only did Halliburton know he wasn't going to follow in his father's footsteps, but he also knew he had to let him know soon. Easter of 1920 would offer the perfect opportunity since father and son would be spending the holiday together in Harpers Ferry, West Virginia. It was the perfect setting for a father and son who loved both the beauty of the great outdoors and visiting places of historic significance. Harpers Ferry was visited by George Washington on his very first surveying trip, was the starting place of the Lewis and Clarke expedition and was the site of the John Brown raid. From 1865 until 1955, Storer College, a historically black school, stood overlooking Harpers Ferry on Camp Hill. Speakers at the school included Frederick Douglass, W.E.B. Du Bois and many others in the early civil rights movement. It was also a place of great beauty. Thomas Jefferson described Harpers Ferry in *Notes on the State of Virginia* in 1785:

> *The passage of the Patowmac [sic] through the Blue Ridge is perhaps one of the most stupendous scenes in Nature. You stand on a very high point of land. On your right comes up the Shenandoah, having ranged along the foot of the mountain a hundred miles to seek a vent. On your left approaches the Patowmac in quest of a passage also. In the moment of their junction they rush together against the mountain, rend it asunder and pass off to the sea. The first glance of this scene hurries our senses into the opinion that this earth has been created in time, that the mountains were formed first,*

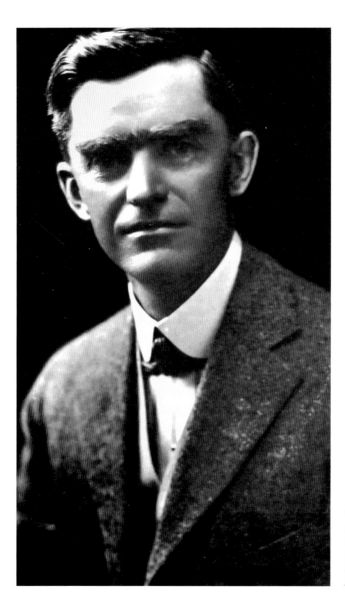

Wesley Halliburton
around age forty.
*Courtesy of the Rhodes
College Archives and
Special Collections,
Memphis, Tennessee.*

*that the rivers began to flow afterwards, that in this place particularly they
have been so dammed up by the Blue Ridge mountains as to have formed
an ocean which filled the whole valley; that, continuing to rise, they have
at last broken over at this spot and have torn the mountain down from its
summit to its base.*[39]

Wesley Halliburton was just as anxious as his son to make plans for the future now that graduation was right around the corner. They began their trip in Washington, D.C., where they met Congressman Hubert Fisher and Senator Kenneth McKeller, both from Tennessee, and then enjoyed a walk through Rock Creek Park together. That evening, they took the train to Harpers Ferry, and the next morning they climbed to a location at the top of the mountain where they could sit and look down at the Shenandoah and Potomac River rapids. Their exact conversation is lost to history, but we do know that Halliburton let his father know he was not going to accept his parent's graduation gift of a three-month summer trip to Europe and instead was going to travel on his own and then write about it. It's unknown exactly how Wesley Halliburton responded at the moment, but there is some indication from the notes in the book of letters he edited and published:

> *This was a surprise. Could it be that a refined, esthetic young man who elected to study the Classics, Poetry, Oriental Literature, the History of Painting, who disliked noise and dirt and banality, could crave to be a vagabond? The father knew his son's flair for travel and restlessness. So after much discussion to develop his ideas, consent was given, with, of course, the mother yet to be heard from.*[40]

It appears that after that day in Harpers Ferry, the Halliburtons supported their son's desire to become a travel writer in every way they could. They provided him with money when he needed it, advice whether he wanted it or not and always a place in Memphis to call home. They edited his work, offered up moral support and, especially in the early years, helped him manage his money.

When Wesley Halliburton used the word "vagabond" to describe his son's post-Princeton vocation, he likely had Harry Franck in mind. In the summer of 1900, while Richard Halliburton was still just an infant lying in a crib in his parents' Memphis home, Harry Franck was finishing his freshman year at the University of Michigan and taking off for Europe on a cattle boat with only $3.18 in his pocket. He returned triumphant at the end of the summer and later bet a fellow student he could travel around the world with no money at all. After graduating, he spent sixteen months traveling the world and returned home to write his bestselling book about his adventures, *A Vagabond Journey Around the World*. Around the time Halliburton was sharing his ideas for the future with his father, Franck had recently released *Vagabonding Down the Andes* and *Vagabonding Through Changing Germany*. When the ultimate vagabond was scheduled for a lecture at Lawrenceville, Halliburton used his connections to arrange to have dinner with him. Halliburton spent days preparing to "pump information" from this adventurer, whom he saw as an inspiration. Of course, when Halliburton's first book came out, he was compared to Franck, and one reviewer wrote, "Where Franck's method is realistic, Halliburton's is frankly romantic as the title *The Royal Road to Romance* proclaims."[41]

Halliburton surely felt relieved when he returned to college after the time with his father in Harpers Ferry. It was also around that time, shortly after returning to Princeton, that he was elected editor-in-chief of the *Princeton Pictorial*. He had already proven to himself he could travel and experience the world on a budget, and with the selling of his first article, he would soon have confirmation he could make money writing about it. His work on the *Pic* would provide an opportunity to learn some of the technical skills associated with publishing and help build the tenacity he would exhibit when faced with a variety of challenging tasks in the future. When Halliburton was elected editor-in-chief of the *Pic*, there were three other student-run publications being produced on campus: the *Daily Princetonian*, the *Tiger* and the *Lit*. The previous year, the *Pic* had the fewest subscribers and was $1,000 in debt. Halliburton's goal was to end the year with one thousand subscribers, get the magazine out of debt and make it an influential publication on the Princeton campus. He kept his parents informed of his progress in the frequent letters he wrote home. It seems an unspoken objective of his management of the *Pic* was also to impress his successful businessman father. Halliburton's letters also show he clearly preferred the production aspects of the publication to the sales or management duties. He wrote, "How I detest soliciting! It's so far beneath the dignity of a senior, and head of the paper, but every ounce of our strength is necessary to meet our competition; so last night in the pouring rain I canvassed freshmen all over town."[42] It seems Halliburton was accused of trying to do too much of the work himself rather than delegating

Opposite, top: Halliburton setting up a photo that would be used on the cover of the *Pic*. *Courtesy of the Rhodes College Archives and Special Collections, Memphis, Tennessee.*

Opposite, bottom: An example of Halliburton's creative use of manipulated photography that made the *Pic* such a success among Princeton University students. *Courtesy of the Rhodes College Archives and Special Collections, Memphis, Tennessee.*

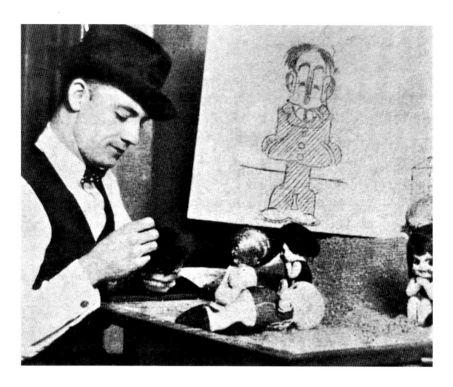

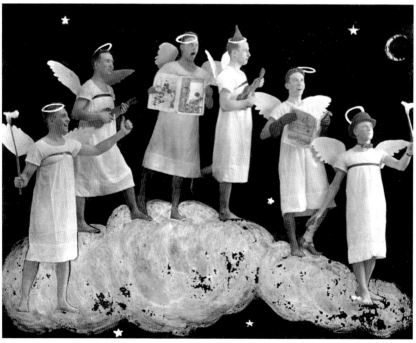

some of the responsibilities to others. During the Christmas season of 1920, he was in a grocery store when a fruitcake tin with artwork featuring dancing elves caught his eye. Thinking it would be the perfect cover for the next issue, he attempted to purchase just the tin without the cake. The store manager initially wouldn't cooperate and was going to charge the full price of $7.50. Showing off his negotiation skills, Halliburton ultimately convinced the manager to rent him the top long enough to photograph it, and he later wrote, "The cry is 'Let somebody else do it, Dick,' but nobody else would have thought of the cake top, or of getting it done if he had."[43] Once, when the engravers didn't have the plates needed to print the magazine, he "stormed" until they stopped other projects and finished his. Then, to top it off, he didn't trust the truck driver to deliver the plates quickly, so he rode with him to the printer. All the hard work paid off, and by the end of the year, the goal of one thousand subscribers had been met, the production offices for the *Pic* had been renovated and the publication was almost out of debt. He wrote, "I've been utterly consumed by the *Pic* all week. Sometimes I think I hate it all, yet when I once plunge in I forget all else but the joy of production—producing something live and worthy and readable. That's the only motive."[44]

As his college years were drawing to a close, Halliburton's thoughts were, like his fellow graduates, turning to the future. What next? Shortly before he graduated, Wesley Halliburton visited his son, and the two took a walk on the shores of Carnegie Lake, in the far northeastern corner of Princeton, New Jersey. Halliburton's father advised, "You've got to make up your own mind, son. You've got to get off by yourself and think things through, find out from your own soul what you want to do, and make your own decisions."[45]

Halliburton spent his last weeks at Princeton attending parties, studying for final exams and preparing for the eighteen-month "vagabond" trip he and his roommate, Mike Hockaday, were planning to take. On June 2, 1921, he wrote to his mother, "I'm so happy here now, more than I ever realized I could be. Even my exams, of which I had my fourth this afternoon, have not depressed me."[46] He later told his cousin Juliet that when he graduated, he wanted to "take one long last look and then run away."[47] And run he did. He left his dorm, Patton Hall, and ran toward the railroad station, headed for New York, where he and Hockaday would find a ship to take them toward whatever the future held.

CHAPTER 7

The Royal Road

June 20, 1926
In four preceding installments Mr. Halliburton has recounted his adventures in many lands while touring the world "on his own." Upon his graduation, from Princeton, he had declined a parental offer of a de lux trip, in order to satisfy an ambition to visit romantic spots without the necessity of adhering to railroad and steamship schedules of such a voyage.
—San Antonio Express

Saturday, February 10, 1923, was a chilly evening in Seattle, Washington, as Richard Halliburton stood on the doorstep of the home where the widow of his former Lawrenceville headmaster was staying. A few weeks before that night, he had sailed out of the Yokohama Harbor, just south of Tokyo, Japan, headed to Memphis after being away from home for nearly two years. He had been told Mrs. McPherson was staying with her daughter in Seattle after the death of her husband, and he was anxious to see a friendly face. McPherson was the wife of the late Reverend Simon John McPherson, a Princeton graduate and the headmaster of the Lawrenceville School from 1899 to 1919. Born in 1850 near Mumford, New York, Reverend McPherson was the son of a farmer and the grandson of Scotch immigrants. Before accepting the headmaster position at the school where he and Halliburton became friends, he ministered at several Presbyterian churches, including the landmark Second Presbyterian Church in Chicago. In 1889, he became the headmaster at Lawrenceville and was soon known by the students and faculty as "a firm but fair leader who was preeminently and majestically Scotch."[48] A proponent of the benefit of sports for teaching teamwork and the importance of physical exercise, he had a state-of-the-art gymnasium built on the Lawrenceville campus. After World War I, returning soldiers brought with them a bug that turned into a deadly Spanish influenza epidemic. Reverend McPherson personally took responsibility for the care of every single sick boy at Lawrenceville, and while other schools and communities lost many children and adults to the influenza outbreak, not a single Lawrenceville student lost his life. Sadly, Reverend McPherson became ill with the disease and died at his home, Foundation House, on January 9, 1919. He and his widow, Lucy Belle Harmon McPherson, had been married forty years at the time of his death.

Halliburton was pleased that Mrs. McPherson remembered him instantly and welcomed him into her daughter's home. Because of the loss of her husband and her close affiliation with Lawrenceville, perhaps while he and Mrs. McPherson sat next to the fire talking that night, Halliburton shared details of his young brother's death and memorial service in Memphis. She might have responded by sharing with him her own early loss and her memory of being a nine-year-old girl watching the solemn parade that met the funeral train for her father to return him to their home, Little Farm, where he would lay in state. McPherson was a storyteller herself, even publishing a book about her father. A close friend of Abraham Lincoln's, when the Civil War began, he helped recruit and form the 125th regiment of the Illinois Volunteer Infantry, for which he served as colonel. He was killed in 1864 at the Battle of Kennesaw Mountain. On the day of his funeral, more than two thousand mourners paid tribute, and flags around the city were flown at half-staff. The sight of Billy, her father's black horse, being slowly led behind the hearse made a big impact on the young girl. But they also had fun things to discuss that night. And other than what Halliburton wrote in letters home, McPherson, whom he called "the grandest old lady I ever saw," was the first one to hear in person the many adventures he had experienced since leaving New York with Mike Hockaday aboard a freighter named the *Ipswich*.

As they would throughout Halliburton's life, personal connections made at Princeton would come in handy after struggling unsuccessfully for two weeks to find a ship that would hire a couple preppy Princeton graduates. The two young men ran into a Kansas City friend of Hockaday's who connected them with Averell Harriman, son of a railroad baron. It was Harriman who made arrangements for them to secure the jobs they needed.

Harriman later became secretary of commerce under President Harry S. Truman, the forty-eighth governor of New York and a candidate for the Democratic presidential nomination in 1952 and 1956.

Halliburton's father would remember being at the dock with his wife as the boys headed out for adventure. He wrote, "We went to see him off, but as the *Ipswich* slowly pulled away from its berth we did not see Richard waving farewell to us, for he was pulling chains and piling wet, salty ropes with tender hands and youthful muscles."[49]

To say Richard Halliburton had experienced a lot since that day would be an understatement. What stories from "the royal road to romance" did he choose to share with Mrs. McPherson that night? Perhaps he told her about he and Hockaday climbing the Matterhorn even though they arrived in Zermatt after the climbing season had ended. After they had been told—repeatedly—that it was too late, Halliburton insisted, and finally two seasoned guides who must have needed the money dragged them up to the top of the mountain, despite the great risk. He could have told her about breaking the rules and taking photos at Gibraltar and then being arrested and put in jail for several days. Perhaps she was the first to hear the story about how he swam in one of the pools at the Taj Mahal or took a steamer in Cambodia upriver to Angkor Wat. He had a lot to talk about. From swimming in the Nile and losing his clothes to becoming the first person to climb Mount Fuji alone in winter, the six hundred days he spent traveling gave him stories to both fill a book and entertain McPherson until early in the morning. Halliburton wrote to his parents, "What a powwow we had! I stayed till after one o'clock…it was a reunion of memories." He added, "When I finally left, she took my hands in hers and said what I knew was true, that it had been one of the most memorable nights, the most Lawrencevillian, most Dr. McPhearsonesque nights since she left Foundation House."[50]

The evening with his old friend probably made him even more anxious to see his parents. On March 1, they arrived at the train station to pick him up after not laying eyes on him for nearly two years. In New York, they had watched as the *Ipswich* pulled away with their only living son, and now they were there to pick him up and take him home. Wesley Halliburton was hopeful his son had gotten this desire to travel out of his system and was now ready to come back to Memphis and settle down. If you were in Memphis in 1923 and wanted to talk to someone in the farm timber and real estate business, you might have pulled out the Memphis city phone directory for 1923 and found:

55

Halliburton & Moore (Wesley Halliburton & D. Moore), Farm Timber & Cut Over Land. 87-88 Dr. D.T. Porter Bldg.
Halliburton Richard, with Halliburton & D. Moore. 1916 Central Av.

When he arrived home in Memphis, Richard Halliburton already had an office waiting. According to family members, there was also a young Memphis socialite who had her eyes on Halliburton and was anxious to reconnect. Richard had wanted to experience his youth before it was too late. He wanted to travel the world and experience things most people at that time didn't even know existed. His mission was now complete, and he stepped off the train that day as a young man brimming with the confidence that comes from making an unlikely dream become a reality. His parents assumed their son would now settle down and live the life they had hoped for him. They couldn't have been more wrong.

CHAPTER 8

Right Time, Right Place

January 3, 1938
This Halliburton who has made the world his playground and has spoken before more than 5,000 audiences got his real start as a lecturer at a New York insane asylum!
—Memphis Press-Scimitar

How did Richard Halliburton go from being an adventure-loving young boy from Tennessee to one of the most popular and well-known writers of his day? First, it's helpful to look more closely at what the world was like as he left Memphis on April 23, 1923, to seek his fame and fortune in New York. He had spent several weeks in Memphis visiting with his parents and trying to figure out what to do next. He had known all along he wanted to write and that a successful writing career would be much easier to launch in New York than in Memphis. After a family meeting, and with his parent's support, he headed east by way of Detroit to pick up the Buick Roadster his father had purchased for him. As he drove from Detroit toward New York that day, he couldn't know just how much the dramatic changes that were taking place at that time would create the perfect environment for a young writer focused on youth, travel and adventure. American popular culture was evolving quickly, and in many ways, the sensational career Halliburton experienced was made possible by the unique times in which he lived.

The 1920s were just beginning to roar, and it was becoming a time of great contradictions and conflicting ideas when Richard Halliburton arrived in New York City that evening. Its the crazy decade that stands between a traditional America the way it was after the Civil War and the modern world power it would become when, for better or worse, new ways of thinking dramatically shoved aside the old. The U.S. census of 1920 showed that for the first time, there were more Americans living urban lives and working in offices and factories in cities than living on small farms or in rural towns. It's estimated that throughout the 1920s, more than 19 million people previously living in rural areas moved to cities like New York. Those two worlds, and what they represented, along with new methods of mass communication, created an environment where books written by a handsome adventure writer who celebrated the culture of youth would find fame and fortune.

Industrialization brought about partly by World War I drastically altered the dynamics of the country, and change began rapidly taking place in many aspects of American life, including work, religion, entertainment, publishing and education. Victorian traditions of restraint, hard work and abstinence were suddenly being challenged, and the results could be felt throughout the country. Toward the end of 1921, there was a short depression. But that had ended by the spring of 1922, and suddenly it seemed everyone living in the big city had money. The number of hours that had to be spent in the offices and factories went down, while salaries for those workers went up. And because America was quickly making the transition from steam power to electric, there were plenty of places to spend that new income. Everyone wanted machines to "modernize" their lives. In 1923, when Halliburton arrived in New York, there were only 27,000 refrigerators in the United States, but in five years that number had grown to 755,000. And the day of the washtub had also thankfully ended. In 1921, nearly 2.5 million enameled bathtubs were purchased, and that number doubled in 1923.[51] With an increase in the standards of living and the availability of more leisure hours, Americans were also looking for ways to have a good time. Broadway, Vaudeville, radio broadcasts and silent movies introduced popular music and new dance crazes with a frequency and speed that had never before been experienced.

During this time, the culture of celebrity was born. Those producing and selling black-and-white silent films discovered that by developing a personality around those starring in their films, they could sell more tickets, and actors soon became commodities to be created and marketed. Around the time Richard Halliburton was beginning his first adventures, Charlie Chaplin, Mary Pickford, Douglass Fairbanks, John Barrymore, Rudolph Valentino, Theda Bara and others were creating in Americans a hunger for information about the personalities they saw at the movie theaters, and a growing number of newspapers, magazines and books made it easy for that hunger to be fed.

More and more tabloid-sized newspapers were introduced, and they were being created for more niche and targeted audiences. Publishers needed lots of fresh content to meet the demand, and those with celebrity status soon included politicians, musicians, athletes, explorers and…adventure writers. Readers were also hungry for advice columns, comics, short stories, gossip, serialized novels and photos, so larger newspapers began buying smaller papers, developing chains that would allow content to be shared across multiple papers in cities throughout the country. By 1920, there were more than two thousand English-language daily newspapers with a total circulation of more than 27 million.

The first news magazines also began in the 1920s. *Time*, *Saturday Evening Post*, *Reader's Digest*, the *New Yorker* and others were launched because readers were looking for better resources to help them keep up with what was going on in the world around them. The "women's magazine" market was cornered by the "big six": *Delineator*, *McCall's*, *Ladies Home Journal*, *Woman's Home Companion*, *Good Housekeeping* and *Pictorial Review*. They offered content women could use to care for their home and family and included articles on cooking, sewing, gardening and travel. Most publishing took place in New York, and an entire culture sprung up around the writers, editors, photographers and illustrators who worked on these magazines. As Richard Halliburton parked his Roadster in a garage and headed to his room at the YMCA on Fifty-seventh and Eighth for the first time, he must have felt a surge of excitement, as jazz music would have been flooding out of the clubs and flappers filling the streets. He was now going to be a real writer, and he was in the right city to do it.

However, Halliburton soon discovered that success was not going to come as quickly as he had hoped. He might have been a beloved son in Memphis and a superstar at Princeton, but in New York, he was just another kid in the crowd trying to make it in the big city. On May 10, 1923, he wrote to his parents, "It's nearing two weeks since I left home. It seems two years and nowhere in the wilds of Asia was I more homesick than I am tonight. No one with whom to discuss what seem momentous problems—only a garret room with 7,000,000 people outside I don't know, and don't want to."[52] The list of publications that rejected Halliburton's submitted work reads like a who's who of American journalism at the time. The Hearst, Bell and McClure syndicates all passed, as did Scribner's, Brentano's and many others. He was trying to sell his book, magazine articles, photos and even cartoons—anything that would allow him to get his work published and to make a little money. During this period, he stayed close to his parents, and letters from home clearly lifted his spirits:

Dad, I get such stimulation and gratification from your letters. Don't let a week go by without one for they have become a sort of anchor for me. The best thing, the thing that helps all the rebuffs, is the joy I take in my work. My fingers itch to get to the typewriter. We'll get there yet—you, mother and I. Who and what can resist our united determination![53]

Although Halliburton wasn't having much luck getting his work published, there was another way a young adventurer with a story could find an audience. Beginning in the mid-nineteenth century, a hunger for more educational and social opportunities occurred, and people began gathering to listen to poetry, watch dramatic performances and hear lectures from experts on a variety of topics. Named for the temple of Apollo Lyceus, where Aristotle lectured to the youth of ancient Greece, the lyceum movement provided anyone with the gift of communicating an opportunity to share information with an audience. By the time Halliburton had stories to tell, the lyceum movement was drawing to a close; however, there was still a strong demand for a good lecture and a host of agents booking all types of talent for women's clubs, community centers, schools and churches. The *Lyceum Magazine* of April 1923 offers a look at who was available for lectures at the time. The selection included Namreh the Magician, who "after two years of preparation offers a big show in a little trunk," and J. Franklin Caveny, "cartoonist, clay modeler and humorist," who was, according to his ad, "a real artist—an orator who thrills." Wherahiko Rawei, Polynesia's most gifted raconteur, was "adept at describing the witchery of South Sea Island life, and duplicating music played by native people." The presentations by many on the lyceum circuit also included slides, photographs or large props. According to his ad, Dr. Rawei appeared in "picturesque native costume" and was "aided by a beautiful scenic background of tropical coconut palms and flowers."[54]

By the end of May 1923, Halliburton was frustrated by the lack of any real progress or signs that he would ever see more than a few photos or stories published. His letters home included the many words of encouragement that inspired him to continue; however, some of that could have been exaggerated for his parent's sake. His biggest fear was ending up back in Memphis in the real estate business, married to that socialite. In a letter home on May 30, 1923, from his room at the YMCA, he wrote:

I abominate this life, but it's necessary, perhaps two weeks more. Things have gone so much more slowly than I hoped for. I get terribly impatient

> at the way my book is progressing. New York has been inhospitable. It's every man for himself here. They trample on those who fall down, but by no means have I fallen down. Things are very much up at the present. My enthusiasm has been given an awful crack or two, but that only makes me more stubborn.[55]

Then, as would happen throughout his life, someone who could make a difference saw something special in young Richard Halliburton. William B. Feakins, referred to as "Pop" by his friends and clients, was one of the biggest lecture talent agents in the business and had hundreds of speakers on the circuit during the lecture season. His specialty was in bringing international speakers to America and putting them on the lecture circuit here. He had entered the lecture management business around the turn of the century when he began booking appearances for a quartet, which included his brother-in-law. From a much different background than Halliburton, Feakins was a native of Yonkers, New York, and claimed to have had thirty different jobs before he was twenty-four. He was very selective about who he represented, and it was said by some that becoming one of his clients would guarantee you success on the lecture circuit. Halliburton went to the Feakins Agency, and, as he wrote to his parents, "for some reason, he [Feakins] was willing to listen." After meeting Halliburton, Feakins did more than just listen; he took him to lunch.

This would be the big break Halliburton had known would come. Over lunch, he excitedly shared the photographs he had taken on his adventures, as well as his idea for writing a book he was going to call *The Royal Road to Romance*. The emphasis of the stories he shared was on "youth" and on living life to the fullest. With a gift for knowing what the public wanted, Feakins looked across the table that day and watched this young, ambitious Princeton graduate with great interest. Halliburton had certainly done some interesting things, and his enthusiasm was evident. International travel was hot at the time. But would an audience buy a ticket to hear his stories? Feakins saw something. He wasn't sure, but he thought there might be something there with which he could work. But he needed to be certain. Ultimately, he told Halliburton to let him know if he got a lecture booked, and he would try to come hear it to see how he did in front of an audience.

It didn't take long, and Feakins must have smiled a little when he quickly received a notice that Halliburton would be speaking the following Tuesday at the YMCA where he was staying. Although Feakins had to be out of town that day, he sent his son, Albert, to check out Halliburton's presentation. The younger Feakins had gone into the family business after serving in France as a second lieutenant during World War I. He knew that if his father sent him to hear someone, it was likely the speaker had shown some kind of promise. He settled into his seat in the YMCA lobby with great curiosity. Halliburton took the floor and tried to begin a lecture on his adventures as a young vagabond exploring the world with no money from home. His voice, somewhat high-pitched and nervous in the best of circumstances, strained to be heard over a banjo playing in the reading room. Suddenly, a bagpiper picked an unfortunate time to begin playing loudly on the street right outside. People strolled through the lobby, listened for a moment and then moved on. Halliburton later said it was the worst ordeal he ever endured. Although the lecture in the lobby of the YMCA didn't show Feakins any special gift for speaking or for capturing an audience's attention, he did agree with his father's assessment that there was something there.

While it isn't known for certain what Halliburton said during this specific lecture, a taste of his early lecture style can be found in a story he wrote for his hometown paper. His father was a friend of the *Commercial Appeal* editor, C.P.J. Mooney, and had shared his son's early writing while Halliburton was still out of the country. Mooney was impressed, and from then on Halliburton could count on the Memphis editor for lots of ink and often, especially in those early years, a much-needed revenue boost. His first article in the *Commercial Appeal* opened with:

> *This story of wandering and adventure is not meant for everyone. The contented, the unimaginative, the lover of the "even tenor." The plodder had better read his morning's paper or his weekly* Post. *But if you are restless, if you have an urge to move, if you find yourself wondering at passing clouds, if moonlight nights have a distracting effect on you, if you love romance and adventure, in short, if you have wanderlust, then these stories are written for you…They are for those who long to feel the touch of salt spray, to tramp in deep northern snows or bask in the starlight of equatorial ocean rolls, and be the first to discover a distant smoke streak and to cry: "A ship! A ship!"*[56]

As Albert Feakins sat listening to Halliburton compete with a banjo on one side and bagpipes on the other, he had an idea of how this enthusiasm for both youth and international travel could possibly be marketable.

At that time, the Boy Scouts was a new organization that was exploding throughout the country in response to the fear that the shift to an urban lifestyle and the loosening of traditional values was causing a lack of moral integrity in young boys. In 1910, from a small office in the very same YMCA in which Halliburton was now speaking, a small group of men put together the plan that, in less than a decade, would result in a mentoring program consisting of more than 32,000 scoutmasters and 360,000 Scouts. Primarily targeting boys from the middle and upper classes living in cities, it also incorporated training in wilderness and outdoor survival because the men of this period were concerned their boys were growing up "weak." This movement to build character and survival skills in boys also spawned an entire subculture that provided services, books, magazines and other materials. As Albert Feakins sat there listening to Halliburton's particularly "youthful" delivery, it dawned on him that this could be the perfect person for a project they were working on over at the Boy Scouts. They were also always looking for good original stories that would appeal to boys for their magazine, so although Feakins held his evaluation of Halliburton's presentation skills for another time, he quickly connected him with the editor of the magazine. After many weeks of hearing his writing was "too young," "too immature" and "not sophisticated enough," Halliburton's meeting with the editor must have seemed like an oasis in the desert. After spending an hour listening to Halliburton and reviewing his photos and previous articles, the editor looked across the table and said, "You are the man we want. You dropped out of heaven to answer a serious call for just such a person."[57] Although the project for which the Boy Scouts magazine editor pegged Halliburton never actually materialized, it was a turning point in his career, and very quickly positive developments finally began to materialize.

After another meeting at the Feakins Lecture Bureau office, Feakins seemed close to adding Halliburton to his stable of talent, but he needed to see him in front of an audience more likely to listen and in a setting without musical instruments being played in the background. He made arrangements for Halliburton to meet with the head of another charitable organization, Charles F. Powlison of the National Child Welfare Association, who created and published exhibit material relating to the "health, well being, and education of children."[58] Powlison used some of Feakins's clients in lectures, and he was willing to give Halliburton a shot on the stage of the Sheltering Arms Orphan Asylum. A temporary home for hundreds of New York's homeless children, Sheltering Arms took in many of those who other organizations could or would not help. Many orphanages in New York at the time required parents to give up custody permanently or wouldn't take children who were not white or who had incurable illnesses. At the

Sheltering Arms, children could stay at the orphanage until their parents or relatives were able to care for them, and children of any race were accepted. Halliburton later wrote, "Two hundred waifs from five to fifteen years old. Powlison and Feakins sat in the back, two competent hard judges…the kids were a tough lot, but I threw myself into it. I told the wildest stories in my repertoire. I acted them out. I knew I had them, for not a person moved. Their eyes were as big as saucers, and I saw that Feakins saw that!"

Halliburton continued working with the Child Welfare Association long after that night, and Feakins became his lecture manager for the next five years.

Much later, Halliburton would tell a slightly different, more animated version of how William Feakins became his manager. As he described the sequence of events for a reporter for the *Memphis Press-Scimitar*, Feakins had failed to show up for ten lectures, so he decided to do something about it. He explained, "I got a taxi, went to Mr. Feakins' office and literally manhandled him. I took him to an asylum and sat him down on the front row." It's possible someone sent William Feakins that article, and if they did, there's no doubt he had a good laugh at Halliburton's exaggeration because no one could appreciate a good public relations spin more than Feakins. After all, that was the sort of hyperbole that ended up making Richard Halliburton the most popular speaker Feakins would ever manage.

CHAPTER 9

Choking Destiny

February 16, 1924
There probably is no human being in the world who can talk with the energy of Mr. Halliburton. He simply throws 'er in high gear, opens wide the throttle and lets go, and for 70 minutes last evening he talked without a comma, semi-colon or dash, in fact almost without taking a new breath.
—Lowell Sun

The end of April 1924 found Richard Halliburton at the Boston Harvard Club on Commonwealth Avenue. Since the previous fall, he had given nearly fifty lectures. His confidence was growing with each success, and he continued to learn from every failure. He evaluated the audience's response to every presentation and tried to figure out what went right and what went wrong so he could continually improve. It frustrated him that some lectures went well while he struggled during others. As he wrote to his father, "I can never explain or understand the variations in my stage presence. One night I am cool as ice, composed, unfaltering, and the next night the lecture creaks and groans."[59] But as he sat there that night in Boston at the head table with twelve old Harvard graduates, he was angry. And the more they complained about how hard the chairs were or how difficult it was to hear in their main clubhouse, the angrier he became. In a few moments, he would be lecturing in front of a large crowd of three hundred important leaders of the city of Chicago, and one of the gentlemen at the head table had the nerve to suggest the crowd had more to do with the publicity rather than with the speaker. Halliburton had grown to accept some initial skepticism because of his age and the fact that his audiences were used to seeing someone much older on stage. But this time, the lack of excitement had nothing to do with his age and everything to do with the previous lecture he had given to the Appalachian Club on Tuesday night. Several hundred "outdoor lovers" gathered in Huntington Hall, which felt barren because it was huge and could have held so many more. The audience gave him a lukewarm reception, and the president of the Appalachian Club had told the president of the Harvard Club that the young adventurer was "bum." Those were fighting words for Halliburton.

Giving all those lectures in the previous months allowed him to hone his craft and learn what he could do to take the audience on a journey with him around the world. Being younger than most lecturers, he was often at a disadvantage before he even began and had to work hard to prove himself to the audience. When he arrived at the Ogontz School for Girls, a finishing school run by the no-nonsense but much-beloved Abby Sutherland, she gave him "a cold reception" before he even opened his mouth. Sutherland was well known and respected, especially in the arts, because she brought the best musicians, authors and other artists to perform or speak at her school. After a long pause, she looked Halliburton up and down and said, "Well…I must say you *are* the youngest lecturer that has ever spoken at Ogontz." To which he deadpanned, "I hope to be worthy of that distinction." Once he began his lecture to the room full of "flappers," as he called them, he couldn't seem to stop and made sure Sutherland and her flappers got their money's worth. Afterward, she told Halliburton, "I know the girls enjoyed it, but while I was entranced myself, I feel two hours is too long to remain in even *that* state!"[60]

Sometimes stage fright was a problem. At a church in Newark, Halliburton had to follow a special program for Armistice Day. That audience included seven hundred people seated and two hundred standing in the back, and he had to get through the choir, prayers, announcements and other commemorative activities before he could even get on stage. He called it "the worst hour of agony I ever went through."[61] Opening for another act wasn't much better. In Brooklyn one Saturday night, he lectured in a theater with two thousand in the audience, waiting to see the main attraction, a Jackie Coogan movie. He wrote to his parents, "There was applause when I left the stage, but a roar when Coogan took it."[62] He presented lectures to theaters packed with thousands of influential businessmen, small classrooms with orphans, old southern mansions filled with ladies of note from the local community and even a group of nuns in a convent. In West Pittston,

Pennsylvania, Halliburton was asked by a club president if he had "brought his poppa," to which he sarcastically replied, "No, I left him home to take care of my children."[63] When he spoke to three hundred presidents of women's clubs from around the country, there was a gasp when he took the stage. Again, they had not expected someone so young. Despite his youth, it became easier and easier to win over almost every audience.

As Halliburton sat there that night at the Harvard Club, his anger grew until it was finally time for him to take the stage. He was on fire, and in his anger, he gave what he thought was the best lecture he had given yet. As he later wrote, "I spat my words out sharp and crackling…if I could be mad every time I spoke, I'd soon be famous."[64] He had made it as a speaker. On Feakins's listing of lecturers he sent to potential customers, Halliburton was now first among the new lecturers and sixth among all those Feakins was promoting for that next season. In New York, he was surrounded by friends and had all the distractions that come with living in a big city. For the first time in his life, he was earning his own money, and his life became a blur of travel, speaking engagements, nights out dancing in jazz clubs, listening to music, attending plays and checking out art galleries. One night at the famed Algonquin Hotel, he and a friend were seated next to Mary Pickford and Douglass Fairbanks, and they watched the two movie stars holding hands during dinner. He would surely have been surprised to know that in just a few years, he would be a personal friend of the two Hollywood moguls.

But despite the money and success and all the applause, there was still no interest from any publisher in his book. In a letter to his son in the fall of 1923, Wesley Halliburton expressed concern that his son would let "destiny choke off the book," to which Halliburton replied, "I'll choke Destiny first."[65]

Nantucket is an island thirty miles south of Cape Cod, Massachusetts. The name "Nantucket" is a translation of the Wampanoag word for "faraway island," and a far away island was just what Halliburton needed to "choke destiny" and finish his book. By isolating himself at Siasconset, a small village at the eastern end of Nantucket, he was certain he would be able to finally finish his first book. He wrote, "I dumped my trunks straight from the boat onto a truck. Sat on top of them. And had myself driven the eight miles across the island—wavery, intensely green, grassy, flowery, but no trees except scrub oaks—to 'sconset.' I'm going to love the place, I know. It's like nothing I've ever seen—tiny flower-hidden doll houses, strung along the beach cliffs." Always looking for a connection to foreign countries, he added, "I overlook the ocean so there's nothing between me and Spain."[66]

Halliburton's plan was to write his book and prepare himself mentally and physically for his next adventure. He could only speak for so long about that first trip. He stayed first in a small hotel room and then in the beach house of his friends, the Buckleys, and spent months typing the first draft late into each night. For the past year, the samples he had shared with many publishers had been rejected, and he had been told his writing was too youthful and immature. Someone had even suggested he leave the philosophy to Plato. But Halliburton had a clear idea of what he wanted people to experience while reading his stories. He wanted readers to "dash" through the book, "not in time but in spirit." He tried to make it read as fast as he talked when lecturing.[67] Although he enjoyed swimming in the ocean, dinner with friends and lots of fresh air, occasionally his old health problems would return—especially when he was tired or stressed. When he felt nervous, his heart would beat quickly, and he often had a lack of energy. In August, after more than three months at work on the island, he stopped for a quick visit at the local doctor's office while in town picking up Mary Hutchison, who had come from Memphis for a visit. Although the Nantucket doctor misdiagnosed his illness as goiter, the combination of a potential diagnosis, the insistence of Hutchison and his determination to feel better resulted in a quick trip to New York to the Life Extension Institute.

Formed in 1913 by social reformer, economist and Yale professor Irving Fisher and a wealthy contractor, Harold Ley, the goal of the organization was to improve the quality and length of life, primarily in white American males. Suddenly, as more men were working in factories and offices, insecurity about masculinity and retaining a level of "manliness" developed. The attitudes about what it meant to be "a man" were shifting. Also, there was a change in the way Americans approached healthcare since many who were living in cities now had access to doctors and hospitals. The Life Extension Institute and other similar organizations during this time promoted changes in health and lifestyle as a way of extending both the length and the quality of life. This was a time when most people knew someone who had died from diseases like diphtheria, typhoid, tuberculosis or, like Halliburton's young brother, rheumatic fever. It was now clearly understood that insects like flies, mosquitoes and fleas carried diseases, and a saying frequently heard in cities at the time was, "A yard of screen in the window is better than a yard of crape on the door."[68] Healthcare reformers wanted to eradicate those illnesses and improve Americans' quality of life by promoting "hygienic living." The book *How to Live: Rules for Healthful Living Based on Modern Science* was written by Fisher and included a foreword by former president William Howard Taft, in which he wrote, "These are the considerations that have influenced me to cooperate with the life extension movement, and to commend this volume to the earnest consideration of all who desire authoritative guidance in improving their own physical condition or in making effective the knowledge now available for bringing health and happiness to our people."[69] The book included chapters on the air, food, general hygiene, exercise and more. It proposed that the path to good health was in being neither under nor overweight, eating and drinking the right foods, abstaining from alcohol and tobacco and the impact good posture, rest and sleep have on overall health and well-being. The book's introduction, written by Fisher, states:

> *Thoroughly carried out, individual hygiene implies high ideals of health, strength, endurance, symmetry, and beauty; it enormously increases our capacity to work, to be happy, and to be useful; it develops not only the body, but the mind and the heart; it ennobles the man as a whole...A great health movement is sweeping over the entire world. Hygiene has repudiated the outworn doctrine that mortality is fatality and must exact year after year a fixed and inevitable sacrifice. It aims instead to set free human life by applying modern science. Science, which has revolutionized the field of health conservation.*[70]

It's likely that Halliburton's physician at the Battle Creek Sanitarium referred him to the Life Extension Institute, as John Harvey Kellogg was a mentor to and friend of Irving Fisher and greatly influenced his writing. After an examination at the institute, Halliburton finally had his diagnosis—he was and had been for most of his life suffering from an over secretion of his thyroid. The symptoms of an overactive thyroid include heart palpitations, weight loss, weakness and nervousness. Many of the physical challenges and frustrations Halliburton had experienced could now be attributed to this diagnosis, and the best news was that there was a treatment. And where was the best place for that treatment? Halliburton was headed back to Michigan and the Battle Creek Sanitarium.

It was there at the old, familiar San where he finished the draft of his first book and then turned it over to his father to edit and to have professionally typed. Feakins had a full season of lectures booked, and Halliburton's health was finally returning. For the next several months, his life was a revolving door of lectures, planning for his next adventure, sending out his book and then dealing with rejection as each time it was returned.

CHAPTER 10

Bobbs-Merrill

1934
Since 1925, when Richard Halliburton's Royal Road to Romance *was published, the Bobbs-Merrill Company has received thousands of letters from readers asking for a short sketch of the author's life. This demand—especially from schools—is constantly increasing.*
—Bobbs-Merrill sales brochure

In the spring of 1924, David Laurance Chambers, having been recently appointed president of the Bobbs-Merrill Company, a large bookstore, distributor and publishing company, sat in his office at 911 Washington Street in Indianapolis, Indiana, and scanned the newsletter he received as a member of the Princeton Club of New York. One upcoming program in particular caught his eye. A graduate from the class of 1921, Richard Halliburton, would be there to talk about his travels around the world. Always looking for new talent, Chambers made a note to suggest that Tim Coward, one of his editors in the New York office, go see what this young man had to say. At forty-six, and having been with the company since being hired back in 1903 as a personal secretary to company president W.C. Bobbs, Chambers had a lot to prove. However, his doctor was telling him he had better learn how to control his temper and relax more or he wouldn't be around to guide the company to even greater heights, as he planned. He demanded perfection both from himself and from those men and women with whom he worked. Always intense and ambitious, when Chambers graduated magna cum laude from Princeton in 1900, he became a Charles Scribner Fellow in English and worked as secretary to Henry van Dyke, author, educator and clergyman. Van Dyke often told friends that Chambers was the smartest man who ever came out of Princeton.[71]

The company Chambers was now responsible for guiding, Bobbs-Merrill, had been founded in 1850 when Samuel Merrill, an Indiana politician and businessman, purchased Hood and Noble's Bookstore and began the Merrill Publishing Company. Merrill was a busy, influential man, and in his lifetime he practiced law and was state treasurer, president of the state bank, president of the Madison and Indianapolis Railroad, founder of the Young Men's Literary Society, co-founder of the Second Presbyterian Church, president of the Indiana Historical Society, president of the Indiana Colonization Society and president of the Indianapolis Temperance Society.[72] After Merrill's death in 1855, his son continued to run the company with a multitude of other partners, which was reflected in many name adaptations through the company's early years. It moved from being merely a footnote in the history of American publishing to huge national success with the release of James Whitcomb Riley's *The Old Swimmin' Hole and 'Leven More Poems* in 1883. Sadly, in March 1890, fire broke out at the business, and a group of firemen climbed on the roof to extinguish the flames just as the building collapsed. Thirteen firemen were killed and others injured, some permanently. In 1903, the final name of the company, the Bobbs-Merrill Company, was chosen in honor of longtime president William Conrad Bobbs.

In the first decade of the twentieth century, Bobbs-Merrill had already published sixteen novels that had landed on the list of America's top ten best-selling books of the year. It had also become the leading distributor of trade, education and law textbooks. The company's role in classic children's literature was cemented with a little girl named Dorothy who headed down a yellow brick road. L. Frank Baum's *Wonderful Wizard of Oz* had first been issued in 1901 by George M. Hill, but when Hill went out of business that very same year, Bobbs-Merrill took over the sale and distribution of that and several of Baum's other books. *Wonderful Wizard of Oz* and others in the series became the best-selling children's books in America for decades. Despite the frequent successes, the one thing the organization couldn't print was money, and through the years it struggled with bankruptcy, reorganizations and frequent downsizing.

But now, things were in an upswing, and Chambers was optimistic about the future. In the progressive 1920s, Americans wanted to appear educated and well read, and they had a hunger for new experiences in foreign countries.

Until now, only the rich could afford to travel, but suddenly with larger salaries, shorter workweeks and improvements in the quality of transportation, people from all walks of life were going sightseeing around the world. And those who couldn't go could read all about it. The purchase of books on travel, history and other hobby-related topics was up, and in New York, Harry Scherman, a former copywriter from the J. Walter Thompson advertising agency, was hard at work launching the Book of the Month Club. Suddenly, people had the desire to read, lots of money and easy access to books. Newspapers, which were always looking for fresh content, now included articles and entire sections on travel and tips on vacationing in other countries.

When his schedule changed and Chambers arrived in New York on the same evening as Halliburton's lecture at the Princeton Club, he decided to join Coward and arrived just as Halliburton was finishing up. Chambers later said:

> *I found young Halliburton going great guns in the final period of the extempore talk. He looked like the Apollo. His light hair made an aureole around his face. His eyes flashed. He was on fire with enthusiasm. Impetuous words, full of life and color, poured from his lips. The effect was electric. His breathless enthusiasm was contagious.*[73]

Of course, Halliburton likely mentioned his book repeatedly during his lecture, and when he did, Chambers and Coward surely made eye contact, each knowing what the other was thinking. Nearly every other major publisher had read and turned down the rights to print Halliburton's book. So while he was certainly glad the gentlemen from Bobbs-Merrill had agreed to read his book and seemed enthusiastic, he knew seeing *The Royal Road to Romance*, as he had decided to call it, on the bookshelves was still far from a sure thing. And since he had completed his manuscript, the next adventure had captured his imagination, and he was planning to follow the path of Ulysses around the Mediterranean.

Halliburton's last speaking engagement of 1925 was in Cleveland, Ohio, so on his way home to Memphis, he stopped by the offices of Bobbs-Merrill in Indianapolis to drop off the manuscript and meet once again with Chambers and some of the other executives there. After a brief meeting, he headed back to Memphis, where, a few days after arriving, he received a telegram at his parents' home at the Parkview Hotel that had been forwarded to him by way of his manager, Feakins:

> *Richard Halliburton*
> *Parkview Hotel, Memphis, Tenn.*
> *Organization enthusiastic about your book and for acceptance if you will cut it up. Shall we send manuscript to you or are you coming north? Please wire reply.*
> *T.R. Coward.*

Despite rejection from nearly every single publisher in New York, Halliburton had still somehow known this moment would come. His father later told a friend that around that time, even though he had been turned down over and over, he was still "absolutely confident, spunky…almost cocky."[74] A telegram from Hewitt Hanson Howland, a well-known editor with Bobbs-Merrill, quickly followed:

> *Became so interested that have been doing some of the work I intended asking you to do. Shall mail tomorrow a number of chapters that will give you a line on the job and from which you can decide whether to give me the gate or the Brown Derby.*

Howland, the son of one of Indiana's founding families, was friends with several Indiana authors, including Booth Tarkington, George Ade and James Whitcomb Riley. He had discovered and edited the work of many popular authors since joining Bobbs-Merrill in 1900. As he worked on Halliburton's book, he was also making plans to take on a new challenge as editor of the struggling *Century* magazine.

Halliburton went to Indiana to work with Howland on his book, and although we don't know if he ever treated Howland to dinner at the Brown Derby, we know he didn't "show him the gate," as Howland had put it. Halliburton wrote, "I've never in my life enjoyed more ten days of pleasant and profitable activity. Indiana gave me a royal welcome. Mr. Howland is an affable, loveable, understanding gentleman. We worked together beautifully. He's keen about the book and gave me almost too free rein to keep it in the singing, capricious spirit I value so highly."[75] Halliburton also enjoyed the company of Howland's wife, Manie Cobb Howland, who was a writer herself and the sister of well-known humorist and New York columnist Irvin Cobb. Working with young writers was often challenging, and Halliburton was passionate about his story and had a specific vision for his finished book. Around this time, Chambers wrote, "One of the trials of life is the necessity of constantly showing an accommodating spirit to authors."[76] One "trial" he had endured was in trying to change the title of Halliburton's book. Both Chambers and Howland disliked it and thought it sounded too juvenile. But Halliburton wouldn't budge. He drew his line in the sand and let them know the book would be titled *The Royal Road to Romance* or nothing at all. Ultimately, his determination won out, and the book was completed and made ready for printing. In future years, fans, biographers and critics alike would note Halliburton's savvy in dealing with publicity, which was evident now, at the very beginning of his career, when he made sure to send a note to be included in the Princeton alumni magazine. All his friends, professors and the Princeton graduates he had met during his lectures and travels around the world opened that issue and read, "Halliburton, Class of '21, Bobbs-Merrill has signed on the dotted and its all over but counting the royalties."[77]

CHAPTER 11

Drowning in the Hellespont

September 28, 1928
One group of American travelers in Europe devoted a day during the past August to the business of out-Halliburtoning the redoutable Richard Halliburton '21, Royal Roadster to Romance and Glorious Adventurer to boot. The means to this end adopted by a group of seventeen college students and one newspaper man was to swim the Hellespont.
—Princeton Alumni Weekly

It was a cloudy day in September 1925 as Richard Halliburton stood on the edge of the Dardanelles River in Turkey, preparing to jump in and swim across. His inspiration for this stunt was Leander, the character from Greek mythology who, according to legend, swam each night from his home in Abydos across this same river when it was called the Hellespont. On the other side was Sestos and the woman he loved, a priestess of Aphrodite named Hero. Inspired by the English poet Lord Byron, who made the same swim in 1810, Halliburton and his traveling companion, Roderic Crane, were even staying in the same cottage Byron had occupied 115 years earlier. After the swim, Halliburton humorously wrote in a letter to his father, "You have the honor to be the father of the first and only American in history to swim the Hellespont. Leander was the first Greek, Lord Byron the first Englishman, and Richard Halliburton the first American."

Although he still loved adventure and thought of every step as an opportunity for something to happen about which he could write, Halliburton could no longer be a real vagabond. He was now a much sought-after lecturer, newspaper and magazine writer and a young man who was about to have his first book available for sale around the country. Different from other trips, this one required a lot of planning and preparation since he had to return to New York before the next lecture season began—plus he needed to quickly experience enough adventures for another book. Richard Halliburton had only just tasted fame at this point, and he liked it. He was also learning a bit from Feakins about the importance of a well-placed news story and how that publicity could increase his popularity and booking fees. In fact, around the same time Halliburton was jumping in the Dardanelles, at his request, a friend in Athens was wiring the *New York Times* to plant a story that Halliburton had drowned in his attempt to cross the tumultuous river.

Months earlier, while working on *The Royal Road to Romance*, Halliburton had decided to undertake this particular adventure. He would follow in the footsteps of Ulysses, the character in ancient Greek literature who, like Halliburton, was driven to travel. Halliburton's adventures would take place in exotic locations like the historic site of Troy in Turkey and the Greek island of Ithaca. No more running away from home alone, the traveling party departing with him for this trip included his mother, who was traveling to Europe as a guide with a group of young Memphis girls; George Gaul, an actor with whom Halliburton had become friends in New York; and Roderic Crane, a classmate from Lawrenceville. Nelle Halliburton and George Gaul went their own ways in Paris, but Crane planned to travel with Halliburton for a few months. It was Crane who was with him at the Dardanelles and who rowed the boat alongside Halliburton in order to record the stunt on film. Back in Memphis, New York and Indianapolis, Halliburton's parents, manager and publishers were dealing with the questions and concerns around his supposed drowning.

Just like when he ran away to New Orleans, Halliburton had supposedly mailed letters ahead of time, making everyone aware that his reported drowning would just be a publicity stunt and directing them to play along. If letters were sent, they didn't make it in time. He later apologized to his publisher, David Chambers—not for the worry his reported death might have caused but for the fact that everyone hadn't played along. If they had, it would have provided "tremendous value for us." He wrote, "Serves me right, I suppose—but I only wanted to be dead for a week to ten days."[78]

There was another book Halliburton was planning to write, and this trip provided the perfect opportunity for research and might have actually been the real reason he chose Greece as the location for this adventure. He had long been a fan of the English poet Rupert Brooke, whose tomb was located on the

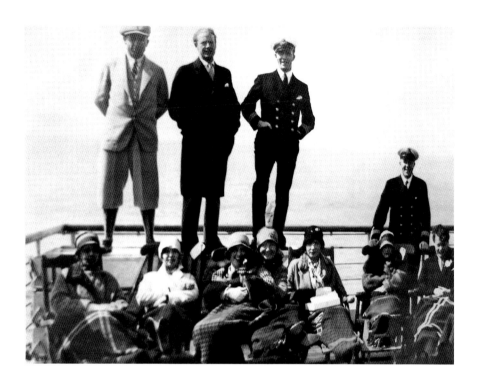

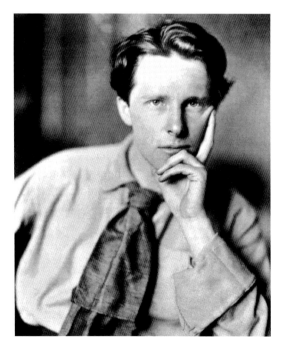

Above: Stage actor George Gaul (standing left) and Richard Halliburton (standing center) with Mary Hutchison (seated far left), Nelle Halliburton (seated, fourth from left), some of the ship's crew and girls Nelle Halliburton was escorting to Europe. *Courtesy of the Rhodes College Archives and Special Collections, Memphis, Tennessee.*

Left: Rupert Brooke, English poet known for his idealistic war sonnets written during the First World War. *Public domain.*

Greek island of Skyros, and was considering writing a book about Brooke's life. Although Brooke was born thirteen years before Halliburton, there were many similarities between the two young men. Like Halliburton, Brooke was from a well-to-do family and attended a prestigious boarding school as a young man. He attended an Ivy League college (Cambridge University) and became famous traveling and writing. In May 1913, Brooke visited the United States, Canada and the South Seas and wrote about his travels in letters published in the *Westminster Gazette*. In addition to his talent, Brooke's charisma and physical attractiveness also helped propel him to a place of esteem among his peers, which included Winston Churchill, E.M. Forster, Henry James, Bernard Shaw and Virginia Woolf. Brooke was known to have romantic relationships with both men and women, and his friend W.B. Yeats once wrote that Brooke was "the most handsome man in Brittan." Another similarity with Halliburton was that Brooke's poetry celebrated youth and sentimental romanticism. Brooke joined the Royal Navy at the beginning of World War I and died of an insect bite on the island of Skyros, where he was buried. Posthumously, he became even more famous than he had been in life when he became a symbol of the loss of young men during the war. Halliburton visited Brooke's grave and wrote:

> *I was a junior schoolboy at Lawrenceville when I read of Brooke's death and burial at Skyros in April 1895. But already I had come under the spell of his poetry and placed him among my heroes. I wonder what I would have thought if I could have looked forward then to the great moment when I was to attain the very shores of Skyros, and on a clear summer night stand before the white stone slab that marks his burial place.*[79]

Before returning home, Halliburton also stopped in England to interview Brooke's mother. About that night, he wrote, "She is much as I expected. Sensitive poets often have such mothers, vital, dominating, strong. She had three sons, all dead; one died in 1907 and two others killed in the war." Although he said he was happy just to meet the mother of his idol, he must have also been frustrated to learn she was not willing to give her approval to Halliburton to write a book about her son, nor did she give him any information that would be particularly helpful during that initial meeting.

While on this adventure, Halliburton also managed to run part of the famed marathon route, become stranded on top of Mount Olympus during a storm and climb the walls of the Parthenon to spend the night among the ruins.

Shortly before Christmas, Halliburton boarded the *Mauretania* and headed home to spend the holidays with his parents and Mary Hutchison in Memphis.

CHAPTER 12

What the Public Wants

May 30, 1927
Born in Tennessee, with the current century, "Dick" Halliburton romped through Princeton University more bareheaded than most, running cross-country, editing a pictorial magazine, taking astonishing vacations by the age of 21. Then he romped around the world in tramp ship forecastles, called it The Royal Road to Romance, *and said he was "living poetry instead of writing it." He talks volubly, cracks many jokes, and threatens to write a novel called* Hell.
—Time

As he passed through the stunning lobby of Mcmphis's new Parkview Hotel, with it's rich walnut paneling and intricate, hand-carved ceiling tiles, Richard Halliburton was glad to be home. It was Christmas 1926, and his parents were now living at their new home at the Parkview. Located on Poplar Avenue at the entrance to Overton Park, it was still a brand-new building, having been completed only three years earlier. Advertised as "the South's finest residential hotel and an address of rare distinction," this large ten-story, red brick building sat on top of what once was an amusement park called "Fairyland," which had burned to the ground after only a few years. Some of the wealthy families of Memphis left downtown for a Parkview address and a beautiful view of the park and surrounding countryside. Halliburton had time to rest and enjoy his family while also preparing himself for a hectic lecture season and writing his second book.

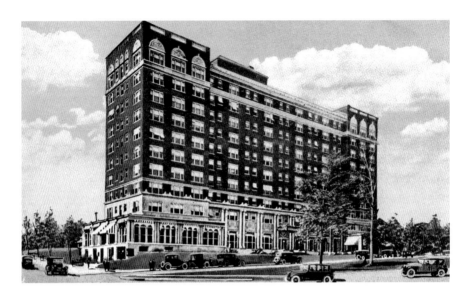

The Parkview Hotel in Memphis, circa 1926. *Author's collection.*

The Royal Road to Romance had been on shelves and in libraries since late October and was slowly beginning to appear at the bottom of a few bestseller lists around the country. Some reviewers who had columns in local newspapers began endorsing the book. For example, Edith Brilliant, who wrote the "Readin' and Writin'" column for the *Sandusky (OH) Register*, wrote that Halliburton's book was "more like a quaff of golden sparkling wine than sheets of black and white literature." She added, "It's not a stilted, where and when book of travel. It's a mental picture painted in words by one whom the literary gods have chosen to endow beyond all hope of a literarily bored world." If that wasn't endorsement enough, Brilliant ended her review with, "The book is well written and it has been highly recommended by Miss Dorothy Keefe, librarian."

A reviewer for the *Salt Lake Tribune* in Salt Lake City, Utah, wrote "Born with more than his share of poet in his soul and the vagabond in his heart...from the platform of the National Geographic society in Washington where the greatest travelers and explorers in the world have appeared this youngest and freshest speaker of them all recently told the story of his adventures and received an ovation from the two thousand super-critical members." Halliburton was also popular in Xenia, Ohio, if you were a follower of Mildred Sandoe, the Greene County district librarian, who gushed, "The book has in it the very spirit of youth. I would have read it myself, if for no other reason than I liked the title. 'The Royal

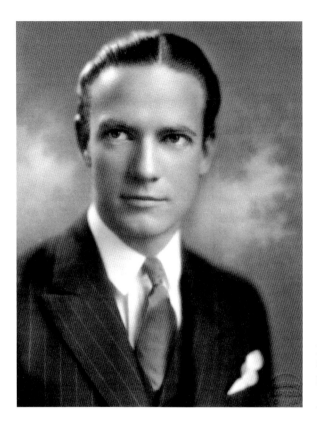

Promotional photograph from the studio of famed portraitist Frank Rinehart. *Courtesy of the Lilly Library, Indiana University.*

Road to Romance!' Hasn't it a gorgeous sound? Now that I have read it I advise you to read it—not only because it has a lovely title but because the book lives up to its name. It is as full of gold and scarlet as the name and if you have any spirit of youth within you, this will thrill you as it has thrilled me."

But not all the reviews were positive. The *Dallas News* reviewer called Halliburton "one of those college boys from wealthy families who occupy the boring intervals between social seasons by acting as amateur international tramps," while the critic for the *Herald-Tribune* of New York growled, "It is a book that lacks the perspective of good taste."

Some readers and critics also began calling into question the validity of some of the adventures included in the book. Halliburton's swim in the pool at the Taj Mahal in particular seemed to come into question more than anything else. In his book, Halliburton had written of his visit to the Taj Mahal and then of the moments at the end of the day when the tourist attraction was about to close:

A few belated stragglers were being hurried to their waiting gharries, and as I saw them go, the thought came to me: "Why not stay?—then I could possess the Taj by myself all alone!" The romantic possibilities of such an adventure captivated my fancy. Quickly I hid in a darkened grove. The watchmen, carrying their lamps, came close to me—but passed on. Not for a kingdom would I have surrendered, with this opportunity before me to remain through the night by the side of my marble mistress.

Then from the entrance I heard the ponderous iron-bound doors groan as they were swung laboriously into place. I heard the clank of fastening chains, and their ominous echo, reverberating from wall to wall across breathless garden, filling me with sudden dread, for I, a mortal, was now imprisoned with a pale pearl ghost—I was alone with the Taj Mahal...Only an insomniac owl watched me remove my clothes, or heard the faint ripple as I dropped into the Alabaster pool. This was a page from the Arabian Nights, *a reversion to the fabled luxury of ancient emperors—this was, at last, Romance.*[80]

The problem came when some critics and readers who had visited the Taj Mahal were quick to point out that the reflecting pools were too shallow for a swim. While Halliburton admittedly threw a coat of red paint on a story when necessary, this wasn't one of those times. It was possible to swim in the pool as he had written. Gordon Sinclair, a Canadian journalist, commentator and author who later developed a reputation for writing strong opinion pieces, had just begun his career as a reporter at the *Toronto Star*. He was around the same age as Halliburton and wrote an article in defense of the young writer after discovering for himself that there were two deep lily pools connecting the more shallow reflecting pools at the Taj Mahal. For some reason, this public support offended Halliburton, and he wrote Sinclair a nine-page letter letting him know that he "had plans afoot for his own vindication" and not to defend him ever again. A contemporary of Sinclair and Halliburton in the 1920s was writer Corey Ford. He included Halliburton's Taj Majal "controversy" in several articles he wrote for *Vanity Fair*. One article, titled "The Adventure Racket: A Casual Inquiry into Publishers Ethics in General, and Several Recent Travel-Books in Particular," questioned the honesty of some recent published works, including Halliburton's, and the opening lines of his article were clearly an intentional parody of Halliburton's style:

Africa! India! China! Borneo! Timbuktu! How oft I have thrilled at these magic names! How oft, as I have turned the well-worn pages of my school

> *geography, have I stared fascinated at those tiny spots of colour that spelt for me the thrills—travel—romance!...day after day I sailed the* Narcissus *toward the horizon—toward the beyond the horizon—toward the beyond the beyond—toward the domes and minarets, the glittering towers, the bazaars and marts of the East—toward in fact the whole vast panorama of first serial rights, foreign rights, dramatic foreign rights, a nice juicy lecture tour in the fall, advertising, testimonials, and, booming in the distance, more travel books to follow—more—more—more. Toward the Royal Road to Royalties.*[81]

The article focused on a number of recent nonfiction books that had turned out to be completely or partially fabricated, including *The Cradle of the Deep*, a supposed autobiography written by silent movie actress Joan Lowell, and *Trader Horn*, ivory trader Alfred Aloysius Horn's stories about adventures in Central Africa. About the Taj Mahal swim, Ford wrote:

> *At least it can be said for Mr. Halliburton that he actually visits the places he says he does. I happened to be in Singapore some time after he had departed, (they had swept up most of the confetti and taken in the bunting by then, and the natives had quieted down a little); and while there were mild doubts expressed there as to the genuineness of his headlong enthusiasm, no one questioned the fact that he had…plunged satyr-like into the Taj Mahal. To be sure, in another section of this magazine, a parody was once published of Mr. Halliburton that meant no offense, but that provoked among other correspondence a statement to* Vanity Fair *from a traveler that the Taj Mahal pool is only about six inches deep and covered by thick green scum. I have never seen the Taj Mahal pool, and I do not know. I do know, however, that Mr. Halliburton deserves infinite credit for having discovered so early and so completely the secret of What the Public Wants.*

Apparently, what the public wanted was *The Royal Road to Romance*. As it continued to creep higher on bestseller lists in 1926, more articles and reviews about Halliburton and his book began appearing in newspapers and magazines around the country. Combined with his packed schedule of now sold-out lectures, Halliburton's star was on the rise. While in Chicago, he wrote to his parents, "Passing Brentano's what should I see but their show window piled with our book and a great poster 'Outstanding Travel Book of the Year' and my picture? We stood aside a moment and watched a score of people stop to have a comment."[82] Halliburton clearly saw the book as a family affair and was working hard to make certain their book would rise to the top of the bestseller lists. The publicity around his lectures generated book sales, and reading his books inspired attendance at his lectures. At Princeton, he spoke to a crowd of 1,500, and the applause after he finished lasted five minutes. In Chicago, he lectured to a capacity crowd at Orchestra Hall and 500 at the University Club. In Bowling Green, a parade of buses and 300 children met him at the train station and escorted him to his hotel. While at Vassar College, in addition to presenting a lecture, he "danced with everybody in the college." In San Francisco, Halliburton was one of the speakers in a lecture series that included Prince William of Sweden; Captain John Noel, who produced a film of a 1924 Mount Everest expedition; and Lowell Thomas, a well-respected adventure writer.

The reviews of Halliburton's lectures that appeared in community papers after his appearances were as enthusiastic as the ones for his books. Mabel Duke, a reviewer for the *Dallas (TX) Dispatch*, wrote:

> *Of all the thrilling, fascinating, cute people—Richard Halliburton takes first place. Can you imagine golden, curly hair that won't lie back straight like its owner combs it, great big snapping blue eyes, one of those thrilling low throaty voices and more pep than a barrel of monkeys—that's he. Dick—who could ever call him Mr. Halliburton?—is in Dallas Wednesday and half the female population of the city was at the various bookstores he visited… He's perfectly charming and witty and has a gift of repartee but—thank heavens—he doesn't wisecrack.*[83]

His appearance in New Bedford, Massachusetts, made a similar impact on the writer for the *Standard*, whose article opened with the headline "Talk Sparkles with More Zest Than Could be Put into a Book." The article included a bit about Halliburton's lecture style:

> *A slender, sensitive, bubbling youth who…came to "get you out of New Bedford!" Humor of the delightfully foolish variety was spilled all through his hour and a half of story telling. Yet he could hold his hearers spellbound by his romantic-dramatic telling of historic tales and of his own feelings when he visited some of the old world scenes he had dreamed of since boyhood. As complete silence hung over the audience at the conclusion of his story of a night alone with the beauty of the Taj Mahal at Agra, he flashed a smile, "There now, don't take it so seriously." His talk was not a lecture. It was just a story of his happy journeying in search of romance*

and adventure. In concluding, he said himself, "I have no sermon. I have no message—but I want you to get out of New Bedford. You'll come back, of course—but go adventuring awhile."[84]

In Denver, the headline "Feminine Hearts Flutter over Romantic Vagabond" was a good indication of the direction for this article:

> Not since Lindy flitted into town has the heart of Denver's femininity fluttered so flutteringly as yesterday. Richard the Lion-Hearted, or, rather, Richard Halliburton, literary lion, arrived in the city for a lecture, a luncheon or two and various what-nots…In department stores, groups of ecstatic ladies—from 14 to 80—gazed on with something akin to reverence…He scribbled his name scores of times and with each scratch of the pen there was a flashing smile or some modest countering remark at cooed flattery.[85]

Its obvious that Rodney Crowther was impressed with Halliburton's appearance in Asheville, North Carolina. He wrote in the *Asheville Citizen* that Halliburton was an "adventurous youth turned loose in a glamorous world" and a "flamboyant young man of the graceful almost lithe figure, sorrel hair, poetical mien and manner." After an overview of the evening's presentation, he added:

> Halliburton is a poet who writes prose: a dreamer who lectures, a lover of gossamer sights and sounds, and strange, almost unearthly places. He is precisely the sort of poetical young man to take desk-chained, hum-drum ridden, work-a-day mortals for a brief spell out of their narrow niche in existence and to carry them whirling with him in a sort of fairy dance through the exotic places mankind has come to invest with the glamour of romance.[86]

Halliburton was becoming famous, and fame was the key to becoming an equal of many of those he had watched from afar. He loved creative people and belonging to the "in" crowd of the 1920s. He was an occasional overnight guest of silent film actor Rod La Rocque, had dinner with F. Scott and Zelda Fitzgerald and was a guest at a luncheon given by millionaire composer Carrie Jacobs Bond, the songwriter who wrote "A Perfect Day" and "I Love You Truly." Thanksgiving dinner of 1927 was spent in New York with Grace Drayton, the illustrator who created the original Campbell Soup Kids advertising campaign, a popular series of paper dolls called Dolly Dingle and the popular comic strips of the day *Dolly Dimples* and *The*

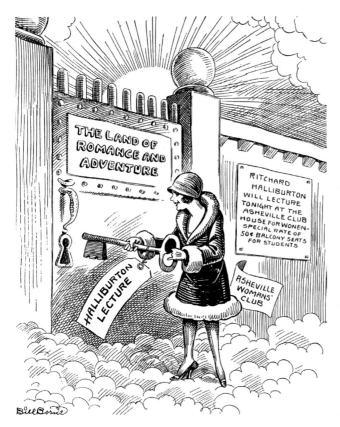

Left: Cartoon from Asheville, North Carolina, showing that a Halliburton lecture was the key to "the land of romance and adventure." *Courtesy of the Rhodes College Archives and Special Collections, Memphis, Tennessee.*

Opposite: A Bobbs-Merrill ad promoting Halliburton's first two books. *Courtesy of the Rhodes College Archives and Special Collections, Memphis, Tennessee.*

Pussycat Princess. Halliburton wrote to his parents, "Thanksgiving weekend in New York at the funny old Murray Hill Hotel as everything else was full up. Thanksgiving dinner with Grace Drayton, alone. We had such a good time. She gets more marvelous every year, quite gray hair now but painting and living better than ever."[87]

Despite the outrageously busy schedule, the parties and the attention from fans around the world, Halliburton was beginning to discover that fame didn't bring the satisfaction and happiness he assumed it would. In July 1926, he wrote to his parents, "I'm lonely. My affections are starved. I've no time to care about people. I wish I would fall in love. It would add some sweetness and sparkle to all the brass materialism. I lead an absolutely loveless life. Friends and acquaintances—too many—all of them could disappear and I wouldn't know it."[88]

In the late summer of 1926, Halliburton was back in Memphis at his parents' Parkview home, where he was hard at work on his second book, *The Glorious*

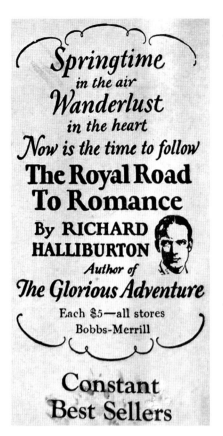

Adventure. Published in May 1927, he dedicated this book to "the real heroes of this story, Nelle and Wesley Halliburton, my long enduring, ever courageous, infinitely patient parents."

The young writer who just three years before had put his own notice in the Princeton alumni magazine could now count on his publisher to buy and place an ad as part of every book launch. It no doubt gave Halliburton an overwhelming sense of pride to see, in the May 20, 1927 issue of the magazine, Bobbs-Merrill's full-page ad announcing the publishing date of *The Glorious Adventure* while trumpeting the success of *The Royal Road to Romance* with the ad copy, "Now in its fifteenth printing, one of the best selling books in America, editions in eight foreign countries." Also included in the ad was an overview of the adventures that would be included in *The Glorious Adventure*:

He swam the Hellespont.
He ran the Marathon—in his way.
He climbed Olympus, Parnassus, and Etna.
He scaled the Acropolis walls at night to visit the moonlit Parthenon and the Marble Maidens.
He visited the grave of Rupert Brooke who is buried on a lonely Grecian isle.
In the tracks of Achilles and Alexander he ran three times around the windy walls of Troy.
He visited the Lotus Land, the Cyclops' Cave, and the Aeolian island of the winds.
He swam—almost—from Scylla to Charybdis.
He braved a modern Circe's charms and looked for Sirens in the caves of Capri.
He followed to their spectacular end from Troy back to Ithaca, the fabulous wanderings of Ulysses with only Homer for his guide and the Odyssey for his book.

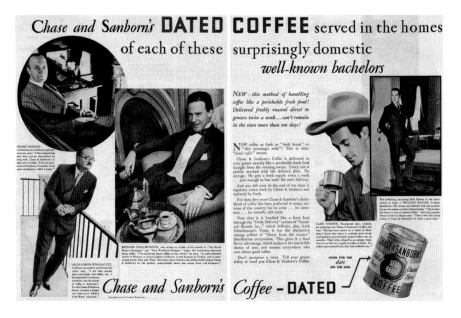

Halliburton's endorsement of Chase & Sanborn's coffee included in an ad featuring "surprisingly domestic well-known bachelors," circa 1930. *Author's collection*.

His popularity with the public continued to soar, so it was no surprise when Madison Avenue came calling and Halliburton began endorsing products. An ad for Chase and Sanborn's Coffee includes a photo of Halliburton reclining with a cup of its product while wearing a tuxedo and looking at the reader seductively. The text of the ad includes a strong endorsement, which reads, "I've tasted the finest coffee in the world…in palm-thatched shacks in Panama, in proud palacios of Brazil, in dim bazaars in Turkey, and in intervening points East and West. But never have I known one which could surpass Chase & Sanborn's for the perfect, indescribable flavor that comes from real freshness."

Along with all the positive attention, fan mail and support from his fans came some insults and criticism by those who determined his popularity was undeserved. Clare Booth, ex-wife of wealthy heir George Tuttle Brokaw, was a highly ambitious new writer at *Vanity Fair* in the late 1920s. One of her first assignments was to write captions for a regular feature in the magazine called "We Nominate for the Hall of Fame." It was Booth's idea to shake things up and introduce a new feature called "We Nominate for Oblivion." As mean-spirited as the name implied, the feature focused on individuals to be held up for scorn. The "Oblivion" article in the June 1930 issue included magazine publisher, early body builder and the father of the health and fitness business Bernarr Macfadden "because he has made hygiene indecent, because his career has progressed logically from biceps, exhibitionism to publishing the raciest stable of cheap magazines now on news-stands"; Republican senator from Utah, Reed Smoot, "because he would rather have a child of his use opium rather than read Lady Chatterley's Lover"; Republican senator from Iowa, Smith Brookhart, "because he has made political capital out of his hosts who have served liquor…and is one of the most triumphantly provincial little boors in the U.S. Congress"; and governor of Chicago and friend of Al Capone, William Hale Thompson, "because he has made glad the hearthside of every gangster, bootlegger, grafter and pineapple artist within his parish." And among that illustrious group, the last person "nominated for oblivion" was Richard Halliburton:

> *Because Richard Halliburton has made a glorious racket out of Dauntless Youth; because his books are marvelously readable, transparently bogus, extremely popular, and have made their author a millionaire; because his invariable picture of himself (patent pending) is that of a diffident, romantic boy; because he is the most popular ladies club lecturer in America, and every knock* Vanity Fair *gives him is just a boost.*[89]

With two books now on the bestseller lists, his public appearances and lectures to packed theaters occurring at a frantic pace, and his name quickly becoming associated around the world with romance, adventure and travel, it was time to figure out the next adventure and book. As Halliburton told his parents, "I'm as worried as never before about my next three years; balancing on top of the ladder is harder than climbing it."[90] His solution about what to do next would come from one of the most popular magazines of the day, *Ladies Home Journal*.

CHAPTER 13

New Worlds to Conquer

January 4, 1930
Rudy Vallee, as a darling of lady patrons of pop arts, has a well-known rival in author Richard Halliburton, who recently visited Cleveland. Halliburton might seem to have an edge on Vallee. He doesn't merely breathe romance in song. He is one who does things. And you know how men who do things appeal to us North Americans.
—Cleveland Press

Loring Schuler had been the managing editor of *Ladies Home Journal* for four years when, in 1925, editor Barton Currie resigned and Schuler was selected for the position as the head of one of the most important women's magazines of the day. Created by Cyrus Curtis in 1883 and edited by his wife, Louisa Knapp Curtis, the magazine, which included serialized novels, short stories, inspirational content and advice on running a home, had already reached a circulation of one million by 1889.

A 1912 Harvard graduate, it was said that when Curtis first began his career as a reporter at the *New Bedford Standard*, he could write about politics but was too young to vote. By the time he took over the helm of *Ladies Home Journal*, it was a magazine struggling to catch up with the new attitudes and culture changes that were sweeping the nation in the 1920s. The magazine might have needed updating, but Schuler would have to do it without sacrificing the significant quality of writing that appeared in each issue. Agatha Christie, H.G. Wells, Booth Tarkington, Dorothy Parker and many other well-respected writers were regular contributors to *Ladies Home Journal*.

But by the time Schuler happened to run into Richard Halliburton in Detroit in early spring of 1928, the magazine was feeling more like Grandmothers Home Journal. Schuler was looking for youth, romance and celebrity, and he found it that night when the two of them had an unexpected late dinner.

Halliburton saw an opportunity to get his next adventure financed but would have to be willing to consider Schuler's request that he write about finding romance in America. Schuler wanted content for *Ladies Home Journal* that would appeal to young female readers who were affluent and interested in travel topics, but he thought stories about America would be more appealing to his audience. He and his staff maintained tight control and offered a great deal of input into what writers were providing for the magazine. While the last thing Halliburton wanted was input into what he wrote and where he had to travel, the lifestyle of a celebrity was expensive, and he needed the money if he was ever going to be able to write the Rupert Brooke book he was planning. Finally, negotiations were completed and his next assignment determined. After much debate and discussion, Schuler, Chambers and Halliburton finally agreed—Halliburton would explore Latin America and write a series of ten articles exclusively for *Ladies Home Journal*, which would then become his third book, *New Worlds to Conquer*. Upon completion of the articles, he would be paid $30,000. In 1928, that was an astronomical sum equivalent to about $400,000 today. As part of the preparations for his adventure, Halliburton purchased as many books as he could find on the topics of Latin America. He sent them home to Memphis and wrote to his father, "Don't be alarmed by the deluge of books. Stack 'em up. There's every book on my new subject I could find in New York. I foresee a big horizon of educational and informative reading ahead for all of us."[91]

The informative reading about Latin America he planned for himself and his parents led to magazine articles and a book filled with interesting stories that attempted to recapture the spirit of the early Spanish explorers. Among the many adventures that would result from his exploration of Latin America would be a seventy-foot jump into a sacrificial well at the ruins of Chichen Itza in the Yucatan, a record-making swim through the Panama Canal and an exposé of the poor treatment of convicts on Devil's Island.

On July 13, 1928, a headline in the *Minneapolis Journal* and other newspapers in cities around the world screamed, "American Author Dives into Sacrifice Well, Tomb of 200, Believed First to Live After 70-Foot Jump into Aztec Place of Death." The story went on to explain how the American author was touring Mexico to gather material for a new book and, while in the Yucatan, "performed a feat heretofore unheard of." Halliburton thought of the stunt

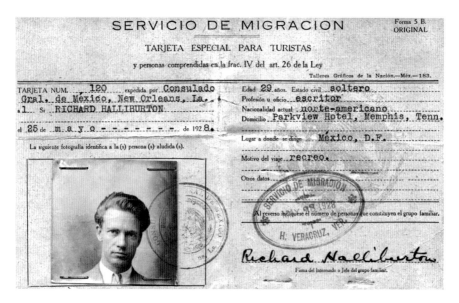

Richard Halliburton's "recreational" travel document issued on May 25, 1928, used as he explored South America for *New Worlds to Conquer*. Courtesy of the Rhodes College Archives and Special Collections, Memphis, Tennessee.

Opposite: A UK advertisement for Halliburton's *New Worlds to Conquer*. Author's collection.

when he came upon the ruins of a well and was told it had been used in the distant past in a ceremony in which "maidens were sacrificed to appease a rain god who they thought lived at the bottom." With a small group of locals watching, Halliburton stood at the well, which was four hundred feet across and seventy feet from the rim to the water, and decided it would be a great story if he jumped. As he later wrote, "It was a thrill as I was dropping down to silent water. The only inconvenience was getting out. The Indians nearly had a fit from excitement." When he thought later of the Taj Mahal and the fact that there would be many who doubted his "well of death" story, he located a film crew and went back and jumped again, this time having it filmed as proof. The footage was a hit back in the town of Mérida, where, as Halliburton wrote, "everybody was terribly excited." Another stunt during this adventure would become one for which Halliburton would often be associated—his swim through the Panama Canal.

Opened in 1914, the Panama Canal is fifty-one miles long and connects the Atlantic Ocean to the Pacific Ocean. The canal cost the United States more than $300 million, and while it was the single most expensive public

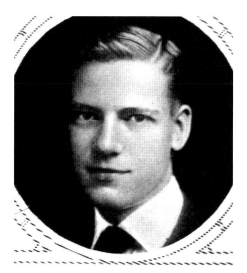

MR. RICHARD HALLIBURTON.
FOR SWIMMING THE PANAMA CANAL AND MEETING THE LOCK CHARGES ACCORDING TO HIS TONNAGE.
Mr. Richard Halliburton swam the fifty miles of the Panama Canal from the Atlantic to the Pacific, and when obtaining permission from the Governor, agreed to meet the lock charges by paying according to his "tonnage" as if he were a ship! The account of his swim may be read in "New Worlds to Conquer," his new book, published by Geoffrey Bles.

works construction project in history at the time, it shaved twelve thousand miles off a boat trip from New York to San Francisco. It took ten to twelve hours for a ship to pass through the canal, and during the process, six chambers that were eighty feet deep were filled and emptied with 9 million cubic feet of water. Ships were raised and lowered as they passed through a series of locks. As expected, the governor of the Panama Canal zone, M.L. Walker, initially objected to Halliburton's request on numerous grounds. But once again, Halliburton's persistence paid off, and eventually the governor provided a letter stating there was "no objection on the part of the canal authorities" to the swim and even gave permission to have a rowboat with a rifleman to ride along beside him. Both Halliburton and Governor Walker knew the public relations value of this swim and even included an element that was sure to be a strong media hook: Halliburton would pay a fee for passing through the canal, but just like a ship, it would be based on his weight. Halliburton got word to the local papers, the Associated Press and the United Press, and by the time he was ready for the actual swim, reporters were gathered to cover the event and dispatches sent out around the world. He was in the news again.

Halliburton played up the humorous aspects of the swim, as can be read in his exchange with the gatekeeper at the first set of locks. Although in reality, the gatekeeper was well aware of the stunt and preparations had been made to get the young swimmer through, that wouldn't make a good Halliburton story. His conversation with the gatekeeper in the book was certainly much more entertaining:

"For three hours you will hold up ship traffic in the Gatum locks. Do you think you are worth it?"

Did I think I was worth it! Was a microscopic earthworm justified in assaulting the gates of heaven and loudly demanding that they swing ajar? Did I think I was worth it!

"Y-yes sir!"

There was nothing else for the superintendent to do but acquiesce. The governor had commanded.

"Very well. But I have this to say, young man. You certainly have your nerve."

Even so, the lights were beginning to twinkle in his eyes.

"One other thing," he added, "before you start blocking the Canal. Don't think the locks are free toll, the governor didn't say anything about waiving charges."

"Quite right, sir. Governor Walker and I agreed I was to pay like all other ships—according to my tonnage. I'm the S.S. Richard Halliburton, registered in Memphis, Tennessee. Length, five feet ten inches; beam, one foot; tonnage, one hundred forty pounds—that's one-thirteenth of one ton."

"One-thirteenth of one ton, eh." He got down his tables. "You're the smallest ship in the history of the Panama Canal." And after a bit of calculation: "You owe me thirty-six cents."[92]

Richard Halliburton still holds the Guinness World Record for having paid the lowest toll to pass through the Panama Canal. He finished his swim in about fifty hours spread over nine days and was accompanied by a sharpshooter in a rowboat in case the alligators or barracuda got too close. He wrote, "It was a whale of an adventure and one not likely to be duplicated. The humor, the sport, the novelty of it seemed to hit everyone."[93] Arriving in Balboa on August 23, 1928, the SS *Richard Halliburton* swam into a large boat slip between the *William S. McKenny* and the *Northern Star*, two battered steamships that had recently been damaged by a cyclone in the Pacific. There to greet him was a cheering crowd and a large number of reporters. The news of his swim was read in newspapers and heard on radio around the world. This was the sort of welcome he would imagine for himself eleven years later when he planned his dramatic arrival at the Golden Gate International Exposition. Sadly, that adventure would turn out much differently.

Halliburton's experiences in South America ranged from the legitimately dangerous to the downright silly, but they all made for entertaining stories. One that also resulted in positive change came from the reaction to the articles written about his stays on a series of islands for prisoners. The most well known, Devil's Island, was located about nine miles off the coast of French Guiana and was among the most feared prison colonies anywhere in the world. Begun in 1852 by Louis Napoleon III, the president of France, the words "Devil's Island" became synonymous with cruel and inhumane treatment.

In the late 1920s, more than 6,500 of France's worst criminals had been sent to live out their sentences on islands with names like Cayenne, St. Joseph, Ile Royale and St. Laurent. More than 1,000 prisoners died every year, and 50 percent of the new prisoners sent in to replace them died in the first twelve months. Death was the only way to escape. Halliburton now knew a good story when he saw one. With no hotel rooms available, he was staying at the local hospital. He wrote that he bribed a prisoner to provide him with a prison uniform and then paid a couple guards to let him spend the night at the prison barracks at Cayenne. He later spent time in a similar barracks on the dreaded St. Laurent. Finally, he convinced the commandant at one of the prisons that he was a famous aviator and thus was allowed to stay in the commandant's home. Halliburton was granted full access, and the stories he wrote of the horrifying conditions he experienced are difficult to read. In some cases, prisoners were chained naked to benches with only a few buckets for using the bathroom. The meat, when available, was rotten and the bread moldy. Halliburton wrote that one way convicts could get a moment of "relief" was to be sent to the hospital on Ile Royale. From running a horse's hair through their skin to cause tetanus to forcing a bean from a castor plant into an existing sore, the extremes prisoners would go to in order to get to the hospital served as testament to the level of suffering that was taking place on the islands.

Because of Halliburton's story, the commandant who had welcomed the "famous aviator" was court-martialed and forced out of the service. Some reforms took place at the prisons, and conditions improved slightly immediately after his articles appeared.

An ad for the April 1929 issue of *Ladies Home Journal* promised an article by Calvin Coolidge promoting peace "in view of European policies concerning limitations upon navel forces," "tested Paris patterns so you can exactly reproduce the latest Paris creations" and excerpts from *Dude West* by Mary Roberts Rinehart, "the world's most noted dude rancher," and *New Worlds to Conquer* by Richard Halliburton. The description of Halliburton's article promised "a glamorous new series by the young adventurer." You could purchase a copy of that issue for ten cents or subscribe for the whole year for one dollar.

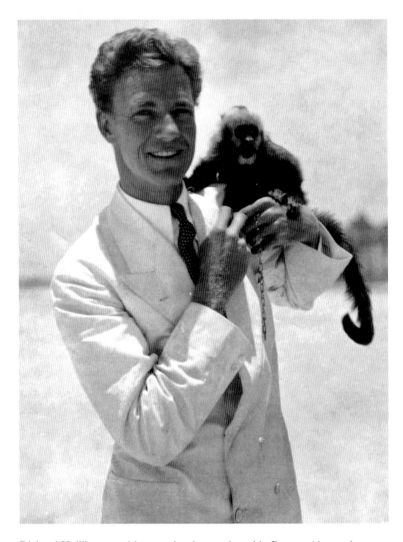

Richard Halliburton with a monkey he purchased in Buenos Aires so he could experience the life of a street entertainer. The story appeared in *New Worlds to Conquer*. *Courtesy of the Rhodes College Archives and Special Collections, Memphis, Tennessee.*

The Bobbs-Merrill Company placed ads that positioned *New Worlds* as the work of a more mature Halliburton, who, at almost thirty, felt the "boy adventurer" label was wearing thin. As with his other books, there were critics ready to offer negative opinions of Halliburton's style. But there was also an adoring public ready to read his book and share it with others.

An article written by Estelle Greathead for the *Mercury Herald* of San Jose, California, is a great example:

> *It would seem as if every enterprising newspaper reporter in search of colorful copy would pack his grip with a generous supply of notebooks and sharpened pencils and follow swift footed the train of that ardent hunter of adventure, Richard Halliburton. If Charles Lindberg, President Herbert Hoover, Ramsey MacDonald and Gene Tunney were all shaken up together they could not offer a tithe of the interesting happenings that befall this venturesome daredevil youngster whenever he sets out on his travels…This daring, fearless, engaging, lovable, and quite irresponsible young rover has the faculty of falling from one hair-raising escapade into another, and of emerging from the very jaws of death with a smiling countenance and pocket full of notes for a new book…The romance and glamour that inheres in history and in legend are as much a part of Mr. Halliburton's make-up as are his keen thirst for thrills, his happy faculty of imperiling his life in every imaginable and unimaginable hazard and his rarely fascinating fashion of recounting his experiences, which has placed him at the age of 29 among the most popular writers of the country with his books having been translated into 14 languages. No one can possibly predict what he will do next, but his admirers are hoping that added years may result in the exercise of a measure of caution, as it is too much to expect that he will always come scatheless through a continual round of death-defying exploits.*

As the 1920s were drawing to a close, Halliburton was among the highest-paid lecturers in the country. He now had three books that were popular bestsellers, his articles were appearing in magazines and newspapers around the world and his fan mail was now delivered to Bobbs-Merrill in bags.

During that period, Albert Milo Shattuck, a handsome, young Harvard graduate from Worcester, Massachusetts, got a firsthand look at Halliburton's life. He had been out of college a short time and working at Gilchrist's, a Boston department store, when he met Halliburton and was quickly offered a position as secretary. Shattuck was responsible for answering letters, making travel arrangements, copying book chapters and articles for *Ladies Home Journal* and taking care of any problems. Shattuck observed, "Every night he lectured and sometimes there was just time to go from one lecture engagement to the next…it was very hard work for him and, as always, he was constantly overdoing. He keeps up on his nerves. When he is lecturing,

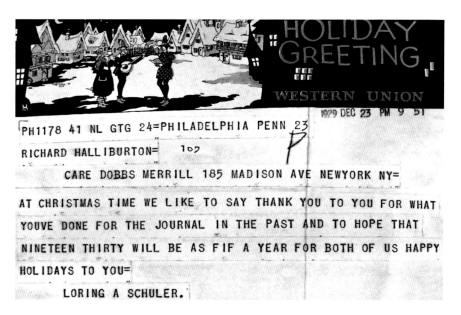

A 1929 telegram from *Ladies Home Journal* editor, Loring Schuler, wishing Halliburton a happy holiday. *Courtesy of the Rhodes College Archives and Special Collections, Memphis, Tennessee.*

he is in a tremendous sweat and uses up a shirt an evening. He writes slowly and laboriously, sometimes doing only a page in a day. He writes and crosses it out and writes again."[94] As someone who was with the writer day and night for many months, it's interesting to hear Shattuck's comments regarding changes in Halliburton's style:

> *His poetic qualities have been smothered to a certain extent by selling. He had a good deal of boyish idealism, and his great admiration for Rupert Brooke led him to visit the poet's family and friends collecting a lot of material for memoirs. But now he says he has passed beyond such ideas. His true romanticism is deadened by the fact that he no longer has real adventures because they are planned out in advance.*[95]

Another of Shattuck's duties as secretary was to answer mail from fans and keep girls away when Halliburton didn't want to see them. The letters, which came from women of every age and from all over the world, were often answered with a form letter that read, "How very sweet of you to write me a letter. In return for your courtesy, I make you a sweeping bow of admiration."[96] Some letters were sent to thank him for his writing and to let him know how much they enjoyed his latest book or article, but some of the women were obviously looking for a husband. Little did they know that a sweeping bow of admiration was all they were going to get from Richard Halliburton. He was not looking for a wife.

CHAPTER 14

Ladies' Man

January 4, 1930
Modern young women seek husbands who will be faithful and dependable in preference to all other qualities. Such is the gist of the comment gleaned from a score of representative young women from various parts of the country who were interviewed on the subject of marriage and other topics. Among celebrities nominated for the preferred list were: The Prince of Wales, Leslie Howard, Colonel Lindberg, Robert Montgomery, Anthony Eden, Richard Halliburton and James Roosevelt.
—Cleveland Press

In some ways, there were three different Richard Halliburtons. First, there was the dashing daredevil adventure writer—an image he created, nurtured and then delivered to the public in his books, lectures and articles. Then, there was the dutiful son who seemed to always seek approval and affirmation from his mother and father and who willingly included them in most aspects of his life and career. Finally, there was the Halliburton who came out when he was with his closest friends or in intimate relationships. While there were some areas where these three Richard Halliburtons overlapped, one area in which the private Richard Halliburton diverged significantly from his public image and his role as the dutiful son was his sexuality. Most biographers now agree that Richard Halliburton was gay. His sexual orientation is of significance here in the context of how a public figure in his era could navigate a very visible career as a "ladies' man" while also living a fairly openly gay lifestyle that included some long-term relationships.

By the time he was in his thirties, although he was discreet, it doesn't appear that Halliburton went to any great lengths to keep his preference for the same sex a secret—and in some circles, it was common knowledge. In a parody of Halliburton's writing style, writer Corey Ford made a not-so-subtle reference to Halliburton's sexual orientation in an article for *Vanity Fair*:

> *How, I asked myself, could I equal this dazzling record?...In a flash I had the answer. I would swim the Hudson River from Weehawken to Forty-Second Street...I chose the same route that is customarily followed by all the other ferries.*[97]

Of course, Halliburton kept his sexual orientation private when it came to the character he created for the public and especially when dealing with journalists. He surely knew that in 1930, the world was not yet ready for a gay adventure writer and that if his private life became public, he would no longer have a career. However, his published work includes the occasional mention of other men who, in retrospect, were most likely romantic interests. In Spain, he met a young American, and during their time exploring the country together, he includes references like the following: "...where Paul awaited me and where, surely, in such December moonlight...almost anything of a mad and beautiful nature might happen." Another time, he made the acquaintance of David, whom he described as "twenty, a good sport, and a clever vagabond whose youthful appearance and manners persuaded his creditors to cancel his debts." After one evening spent with his new friend, Halliburton wrote, "David and I will not soon forget the first night we spent in the capital. True, it was spent mostly in our beds, but they were out in the lilac garden..."

Halliburton also had many relationships with other gay men who were public figures and therefore understanding of his need for discretion. John van Druten, an English playwright and theater director, invited Halliburton to stay with him at his home on the Isle of Skye in Scotland. When the two met, van Druten was enjoying "overnight" success in New York from the rave reviews and popularity of one of his earliest plays, *Young Woodly*. As Halliburton wrote his parents, "A wire came to me at Montreal from John van Druten saying he'd be in the Hebrides and a letter awaited me at the boat urging me to join him at Skye. I've always wanted to visit the Hebrides—they sound so lonely and romantic—so I'm going there tomorrow and get on to London by the ninth."[98] Another interesting friend with whom Halliburton became very close was Noël Sullivan. From a very wealthy San

Francisco family, Sullivan was the nephew of Senator James D. Phelan and a significant supporter of the arts. His home on Hyde Street, in San Francisco, was an early gathering place for many musicians, artists and writers.

Although his friends didn't care who he slept with, Halliburton did have to explain to the press why America's favorite playboy was still a bachelor. As biographer Gerry Max wrote, "Halliburton promoted the image of himself, always fearful of risking the exposure that might alienate him from a public comprised chiefly of adoring women who swooned over him…and of young men who saw in him a beacon of romantic adventure."[99] It also seems Halliburton, always the talented press agent, never missed an opportunity to reinforce the image he wanted projected, especially when the topic was marriage. In an interview with Marion Lealand for the *Brooklyn Eagle*, he explained why he was still single:

> *Richard Halliburton, blondly handsome, athletically built and esthetically poised, gaily youthful and determinedly flippant yet unashamedly gallant withal…but he solemnly confessed that he isn't in love and hasn't been but only because he doesn't have time enough in which to meet the young maidens who might easily capture his fancy if only there were time for a second meeting. "You know," he confessed, "I've been lecturing for years and years and when I'm not doing those other things like swimming the Hellespont or climbing Mount Aeolus its always a case of rushing about from one place to another." Dick is quite sure he'd have fallen in love and then married by now and everything if he'd only have had opportunity to say "hello" twice to some of the beautiful girls he's always meeting.*[100]

When asked about his ideal woman by writer Dorothy Dayton, Halliburton took the opportunity to reinforce for her readers his connection to both travel and youth. In the 1930 article written for the *Illustrated Love* magazine, he told Drayton, "My ideal girl…can twirl a fan like a woman I saw in Peru. She has a little of the Japanese maid's fragile charm. She walks like a girl in Bali, and she has eyes like a woman in Kashmir…and like the American girl, she keeps her youth for a long time."[101]

He gave a more candid interview about women in an article written for *The Home* magazine by Myriam Sieve, in which she brought together four "remarkable" men for a series called "The Tea Table Debate." Sieve brought the men together and led the discussion, but mostly she sat back, let the men talk and then reported the conversation. In addition to Halliburton, the diverse group included Tony Sarg, an illustrator and artist who introduced modern puppetry in America; Joseph P. McEvoy, humorist, writer and creator of *Dixie Dougan*, a long-running syndicated comic strip; and Dr. Abraham A. Brill, the psychiatrist who first translated Freud into English.

In the article, Sieve described Halliburton as being "rather shorter and slighter than one expects" and having "the ruddy complexion of an outdoor person and extremely good-looking." In addition to discussing attitudes of "modern young men" and whether the standards for college graduates have risen, the topic of men and women came up. After Dr. Brill suggested that men were like a motor and women like the fuel required to make the motor run, the conversation continued:

> *"Don't you think the motor is becoming more and more able to function without fuel?"* asked Halliburton.
> *"So far it has not,"* returned the psychiatrist.
> *"Why is it that more men are content to live alone?"* persisted the writer.
> *"They live alone in the sense that they do not marry,"* said Dr. Brill, *"but they must have a woman to stimulate them to action. I'm talking, of course, of the average young men."*
> *"What about colleges and monasteries?"* Mr. Halliburton argued.
> *"Colleges are not monasteries,"* replied Dr. Brill.[102]

Elsewhere in the article, the men debated whether men or women were more aggressive. Halliburton said, "It has been my experience that women are more forward—more brazen than men. For instance, I do a lot of speaking in boys' and girls' schools. When they come down to the platform to speak to me afterwards, the boys don't have a chance, for the girls crowd forward and the boys are shy and hang back. Women always do that."[103]

In the early letters between Halliburton and his parents, there were discussions regarding some of the young women with whom he spent time, but he always assured his parents there was nothing serious happening. Wesley Halliburton was also anxious for grandchildren, and at times his son made an occasional comment that possibly gave him hope that the "right girl" was going to come along.

In his third book, *New Worlds to Conquer*, Halliburton included a possible metaphor for his own life in a storyline about a young woman named Isabella. She didn't make fun of his style of swimming like others who were watching. Halliburton wrote, "She seemed to understand that I was a land animal doing my best to be a dolphin, and she appreciated the difficulties I was having."

CHAPTER 15

Flying Carpet

November 26, 1932
The Playboy of Romance; Radio and Advertising…The playboy of high and galumphing romance, Old Dick Halliburton, is at it again, this time flying his magic carpet literally and every which way to all the lurid ports of imagination's call in the world. When this fellow gets to be past 40 (if ever) we recommend that Mr. Howard or Mr. Ochs or Mr. Hearst pick him up as a roving correspondent extraordinaire and let the penny customers in on a rare feast of reportorial imagination.
—*clipping from unidentified movie magazine*

Mark Sullivan, a journalist and social observer of the history and culture of the early twentieth century, wrote, "Of all the agencies that influenced man's mind that made the average man of 1925 intellectually different from him of 1900, by far the greatest was the sight of a human being in an airplane."[104] The Wright brothers first took off and flew at Kill Devil Hills, North Carolina, on December 17, 1903. While they introduced a new form of transportation, they also began an entirely new aspect of the culture of the early twentieth century. Aerial exhibitions around the country became a popular spectator sport as men and women risked their lives, and many times lost them, demonstrating that it really was possible for man to fly. Many women saw flying as a way to express their equality to men at a time when they had only recently begun voting. Pilots of both sexes became equal to the most well-known and popular celebrities of the day, and their feats were covered in newspapers and magazines, on the radio and in newsreels shown in movie theaters around the world. Everyone had gone airplane crazy. Dominick Pisano included in *The Airplane in American Culture* a passage that well conveys the emotion behind the concept of flight that occurred for many of that period:

> *Indeed to many people, the swift, high-flying airplane epitomized the promise of the technological age. Driving to the airfield to watch the preparations for the 1927 transatlantic flights, the essayist and literary critic Gilbert Seldes followed the highway through a gritty, bleak industrial area, succeeded, in turn, by the "tasteless monotony" of colonies of worker's homes. It left him depressed until suddenly he reached the flying field. An airplane possessed a fragility and grace—and dazzling speed to whisk it over the horizon. A dwindling speck, it turned; a polished surface of the wing reflected a waning ray of daylight like a window flaming in the setting sun. An aircraft embodied an anomaly of prosaic notations of equations, wood, fabric, engine, and gasoline that produced the wonder and thrill of throwing off the bonds of the earth.*[105]

On May 20, 1927, Charles Lindbergh took flight in the *Spirit of St. Louis* from Roosevelt Field, near New York City, at 7:52 a.m. When he landed at Le Bourget Field, near Paris, just thirty-three hours and thirty minutes later, he had flown more than thirty-six thousand miles and had become, for that moment, the most famous man in the world. He was honored with parades, celebrations and parties, and news media around the world suddenly reported every move he made. He was even given the Congressional Medal of Honor and the Distinguished Flying Cross by President Calvin Coolidge. Halliburton watched with a touch of envy.

Around this time, *The Glorious Adventure* was just appearing in bookstores, *The Road to Romance* was still topping the charts and Halliburton was spending that summer in Europe researching Rupert Brooke for the book he planned to write. Reading the newspapers and hearing the news coverage on the radio, the seeds of an idea were planted; his next adventure would happen on an airplane.

Just two years later, the Great Depression had hit the country, and sales of Halliburton's third book, *New Worlds to Conquer*, were leveling out at just thirty thousand copies—still a bestseller, but not coming close to the sales of his first two books. Halliburton headed to Hollywood to negotiate the movie rights for *The Royal Road to Romance* to add some much-needed revenue to his bank account. Although he made a lot of money from his books and lectures, he also enjoyed the lifestyle of a celebrity and found great pleasure in helping his friends and family—and that took lots of money. Additionally, the depression had hit his parents back in Memphis hard, and it was he who was now sending money home to them. Mary Hutchison was also working hard to keep the doors of her school open. In 1925, she, along with Wesley Halliburton and four other Memphis businessmen, formed a corporation and issued bonds to build a new school at 1925 Union Avenue. Although times were lean, Hutchison's school stayed open during the difficult years of the 1930s, when many other private schools around the nation closed.

Once the negotiations were complete, Fox and Halliburton agreed to the sum of $15,000, and Halliburton was now in need of another adventure. Both Schuler at *Ladies Home Journal* and Chambers at Bobbs-Merrill responded favorably to his idea of capitalizing on the latest trend by writing about an adventure taken in an airplane. Halliburton wired his parents, asking them to come to Hollywood as soon as possible. Once they arrived, he presented his ideas for "their" next adventure. He felt stories written about travel in an airplane would allow him to maintain the public's perception of him as a daring explorer and give him fresh, contemporary experiences about which he could write. According to Halliburton's father, although they were afraid for their son, after "several day's discussion and analysis," they agreed not to oppose what Wesley Halliburton referred to as "such an unusual enterprise."[106]

In the fall of 1930, pilot Moye Stephens was waiting to meet Richard Halliburton at the glamorous new Roosevelt Hotel at 7000 Hollywood Boulevard in Los Angeles. Financed by a group that included Douglas Fairbanks, Mary Pickford and Louis B. Mayer, the elegant hotel still had that fresh paint and new carpet smell, and it had become the hot spot frequented by everybody who was anybody in the movie business in 1930. Just months earlier, it had been the site of the very first Academy Awards presentation. Although only twenty-four years old, Stephens had already had his commercial pilot's license for eight years and was considered a leader in the aviation field. In order to make his father happy, he graduated from Stanford University with a major in law, but his real love was flying, so he left law behind and moved on to a career as a pilot. While attending college, Stephens worked as a stunt pilot for movies like Cecil B. DeMille's *Corporal Kate* and Howard Hughes's *Hell's Angels*. With movie star good looks and a calm, patient demeanor, he was also a popular flying instructor, giving many in Hollywood, including Howard Hughes, their first flying lessons. When he received the call from Halliburton requesting a meeting, Stephens was flying for Transcontinental Air Transport and had recently been elected president of the Professional Pilots Association. With the respect of his peers, proven integrity and years of experience flying airplanes, a pilot like Stephens was just who Halliburton needed to fly him around the world.

Since starting this new adventure, Halliburton had already been taken advantage of twice. First, someone claiming to be a former Royal Air Force pilot talked him into providing $500 as seed money for a transatlantic flight and then disappeared once the money was deducted from future royalties and wired to his hotel by Bobbs-Merrill. Then, he began working with a second pilot who was a "highly-decorated Marine." After using Halliburton's money to purchase an airplane for the trip, a friend in the aviation field pointed out to Halliburton that his new pilot, although possessing some impressive medals, had incorrectly attached them to his uniform. After further investigation by Halliburton's insurance provider, it was determined that his new pilot was never a marine, nor did he have even a minute of solo flight time. Halliburton desperately needed a pilot he could trust, and a sympathetic friend gave him Stephen's name and suggested he give him a call.

As they sat together in the lobby of the luxurious hotel, with Halliburton sharing his idea for an adventure around the world in an airplane, Stephens watched the enthusiastic and energetic author closely. He later wrote, "My first impression of Halliburton was one of surprise at the slight build and medium height of the boyishly handsome, vibrant young man. His lack of a robust physique was compensated for by a remarkable fund of nervous energy and dogged determination."[107]

Halliburton pitched the idea with great flourish. The two could fly anywhere in the world, stay as long as they were having fun and then take off for another destination. It was an intriguing offer for a young man who had already accomplished much in the field of aviation, but one that would require a great deal of consideration. Stephens would have to quit his job as a pilot and be willing to leave the country for up to two years. After several meetings and long discussions about the plan, Stephens finally agreed, but with several stipulations. Wisely, he didn't want to be considered an employee of Halliburton's but rather a traveling companion with equal billing. Instead of a salary, Stephens would receive an unlimited expense account with few obligations beyond getting the plane safely from one point to the next and managing the financial records. Halliburton's outgoing lifestyle and sexual orientation was not a secret in Hollywood, and the conservative Stephens also required an agreement that he and Halliburton would have separate rooms and that he not be required to attend any "social functions" or make

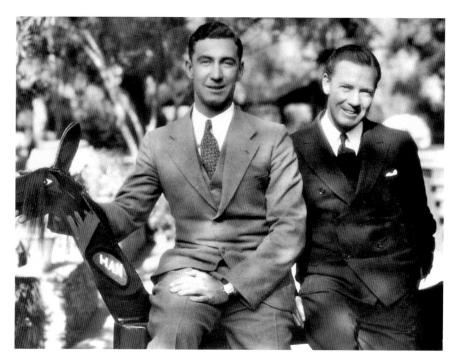

Moye Stephens and Richard Halliburton. *Courtesy of Moye F. Stephens.*

Opposite, top: Halliburton, Stephens and Novarro in a photo taken by Hollywood glamour photographer George Hurrell. *Courtesy of Moye F. Stephens.*

Opposite, bottom: Pancho Barnes poses with Stephens and Halliburton in this photo taken by Hollywood glamour photographer George Hurrell. *Courtesy of Moye F. Stephens.*

any public speeches. Finally, after he checked out Halliburton's new airplane, he added a requirement that a new one for the journey was nonnegotiable.

Not surprisingly, the airplane that Halliburton's phony pilot had purchased was not suitable for this type of trip and was actually in very bad shape. Having survived a crash, it had been poorly reassembled and would never have survived even a short trip. Because of his anxiousness to get this adventure started, Halliburton had clearly put himself in great danger, which easily could have resulted in his death. After much research and consideration, Stephens selected a Stearman C-3B for the adventure. An American-built civil biplane designed by Stearman Aircraft of Wichita, Kansas, the plane had an open cockpit with room for two passengers and all their gear and was built for taking off and landing in rough terrain.

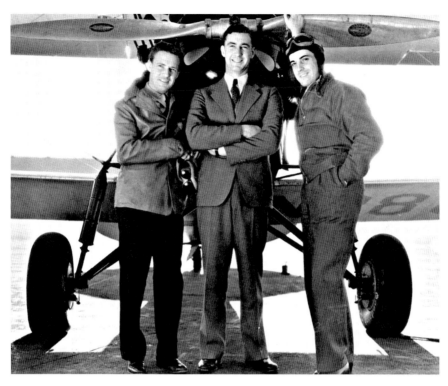

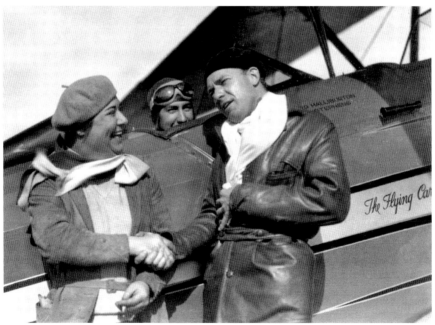

Halliburton named their airplane the *Flying Carpet*, and the two began earnestly preparing for their trip around the world.

Both Stephens and Halliburton were well liked in Hollywood and, between the two of them, knew pretty much everyone in town in the aviation and movie businesses. In the weeks leading up to their departure, Stephens took Halliburton to a party hosted by his friend, the fascinating female pilot Florence "Pancho" Barnes. They had worked together on *Hell's Angels*, and Stephens thought she would be the sort of character Halliburton could appreciate. He was right.

Barnes had grown up in a wealthy family in Pasadena, California, but as a tomboy who preferred to hunt and ride horses rather than attend afternoon tea parties, she didn't fit the model of a Southern California socialite. After a childhood spent struggling with her parents over her free spirit and determination to do things her own way, her mother convinced her to wed a much older Episcopal minister named Rankin Barnes. Although they did have a son together, it was an unhappy marriage. In future years, Pancho would tell friends that as far as she was concerned, her son was a virgin birth. The reverend refused to give his wife a divorce, so as a way of occupying herself and getting away from what she considered the boring life of a preacher's wife, she began a career working with horses that were being used in silent films.

Barnes continued looking for ways to escape and eventually joined friends on a ship that they later discovered was running guns and ammunition to revolutionaries in Mexico. Barnes had cut her hair short and sometimes disguised herself as a man during the adventure. When she returned to Pasadena, she wanted to be called "Pancho," the nickname given her in Mexico, and she began taking flying lessons. According to legend, during her first solo flight, she buzzed over her husband's church, creating a disturbance during his Sunday morning sermon. Reporters began referring to Pancho Barnes as the "high-society aviatrix," and she was Halliburton's equal when it came to using the power of the media to create a controversial public image. Halliburton biographer Gerry Max wrote, "Barnes went against type, appearing more a grown-up version of one of the Little Rascals than to the manor born. Though a 'society dame,' the designation didn't quite fit the cigar-whiffing, middle-finger saluting and four-letter flinging Florence Barnes."[108] Moye Stephens described Barnes as also having "a heart as big as the great outdoors" and said she would "take in stray puppies, or anything of that nature." When she and Halliburton first met, Barnes had recently participated in the Powder Puff Derby, in which female pilots raced from Santa Monica, California, to Cleveland, Ohio. Organized by famous aviatrix Bobbi Trout, the race also featured Amelia Earhart. Ironically, one of the biggest enemies of female pilots and a vocal critic of the Powder Puff Derby was Richard Halliburton's millionaire cousin, Erle Halliburton.

Pancho Barnes operated one of the earliest flying circuses and, when she met Halliburton, was living in Hollywood working as a stunt pilot for movies. Generous with her dwindling inheritance, Barnes's nightly parties at her San Marino mansion were legendary among Hollywood aviators, celebrities, musicians and others in the movie business, and it was likely at such a gathering that Halliburton met Ramón Novarro and possibly Paul Mooney. Novarro had become the hottest male screen star in Hollywood after achieving great success in the epic film *Ben-Hur: A Tale of the Christ*. He and Barnes were close friends, and after they met, he and Halliburton became close as well. The two might have been romantically involved for a time, but it was Mooney who would figure most prominently in Halliburton's future. He was, like Halliburton, a writer looking for a life of adventure, and the two hit it off immediately. It's possible they had met earlier since they ran in the same social circles and were acquainted with many of the same people. Regardless of exactly when and where they met, once they connected, other than his parents, Mooney was the person to whom Halliburton would become the closest in the final years of his life.

Halliburton and Moye spent a few days in late December 1930 in Memphis before departing for their adventure around the world. Moye wrote to his parents from Memphis, "Beginning with the night we arrived, we have been to one and sometimes two parties every night and also quite a few in the afternoons. Needless to say, Dick is a very large big shot in his home town—their fair-haired boy."[109] Halliburton's parents and Memphis friends gathered at the airport to see them off the first week of January 1931.

The moment the *Flying Carpet* took off, it marked for Wesley Halliburton a distinct moment in which he realized the relationship with his son would never again be the same. He wrote a letter to his son sharing that realization and then, much later in life, showed the letter to his friend and writer James Cortese, who included this recollection of it in his own book about the Halliburtons:

Dear Richard:

As I stood watching the Flying Carpet *grow smaller and smaller, to finally disappear into the distant haze, I felt something new, some strange, deep emotion I have never experienced before. No, it was not fear for you or your plane and crew—I know you can take care of yourself; you are now a man, grown up, self sufficient, able—I am proud of you. No, it is not that—it is something entirely different that I have not felt when you departed from us before. It is, I think, that for the first time I realize that you no longer belong to your mother and me. You now belong to your readers, your vast audience—you belong to the world.*[110]

A few weeks later, Halliburton wrote his parents that he thought his father's letter was a "masterpiece" and said he was "sending it back home to be put away for his grandchildren to read." No doubt a curious response considering the situation, it was likely meant to be a consolatory gesture from a son who held his parents in such high regard. He really wanted to please his father, and if that meant providing grandchildren, perhaps he thought someday he would.

By the time Halliburton and Stephens completed their journey on June 2, 1932, they had been away from home eighteen months. Together they had logged 374 hours flying over thirty-four countries, traveled more than thirty-three thousand miles and experienced 178 landings.[111] They flew over deserts and jungles, up the sides of the world's tallest mountains and inside volcanic craters. Halliburton spent around $50,000 during the trip and returned home completely broke. He arrived back in the United States and was greeted with letters from his banker in New York letting him know he was $2,000 overdrawn.

Their early experiences during the journey included a stay in Timbuktu, a three-hundred-year-old former slave-trading marketplace in the West African nation of Mali, and then some time serving in the French Foreign Legion. Halliburton had written a story about each adventure and sent them off to Schuler at *Ladies Home Journal*, but when a response was slow in coming, he panicked. Throughout the trip, he would have periods of extreme anxiety, caused by fear that what he was writing wouldn't be interesting or that he had lost his touch and that the economic depression had changed the public's appetite, rendering him irrelevant. At their stops across Europe,

---

Opposite, top: Mary Hutchison with Wesley and Nelle Halliburton while reading one of Richard Halliburton's letters. *Courtesy of the Rhodes College Archives and Special Collections, Memphis, Tennessee.*

Opposite, bottom: Halliburton and Moye Stephens with the *Flying Carpet*. *Courtesy of the Rhodes College Archives and Special Collections, Memphis, Tennessee.*

A High-Flying Life from Tennessee to Timbuktu

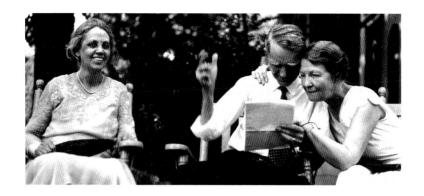

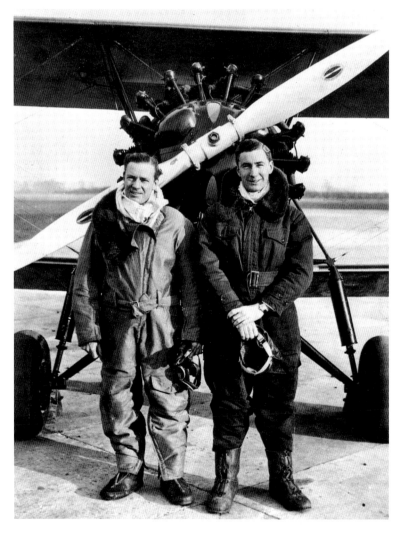

> TELEGRAMS:-
> MAHARAJA, RAXAUL.
>
> Galstaun Park
> Calcutta
> TANGAL DURBAR,
> NEPAL.
>
> 6th January 1932.
>
> Dear Mr. Haliburton,
>
> Permit me please to tell you how very much we enjoyed the demonstration in flying shown by you in your plane and how greatly we appreciated the goodness which made you give us such a nice treat. I am indeed much obliged to you for that and write to offer you once more very many thanks.
>
> With every good wish,
> Yours truly,
>
> Maharaja, Nepal.
>
> To,
> Mr. Haliburton
> Great Eastern Hotel
> Old Court House Street
> Calcutta

Halliburton and Stephens were wined and dined by the local politicians and social elite in each community. They took the sixteen-year-old crown prince of Iraq for a ride up the Tigris to Samarra, where they enjoyed lunch fit for a future king on the steps of an ancient mosque. They spent time with the family of the late "White Rajah," James Brooke, in Kuching, the capital of Sarawak, on the island of Borneo and joined the Calcutta Flying Club in an air show for the Maharajah of Nepal. They followed the route of the Christian Crusaders and soared high above the Taj Mahal. Always frustrated about the accusations that he had lied about his story of swimming in the

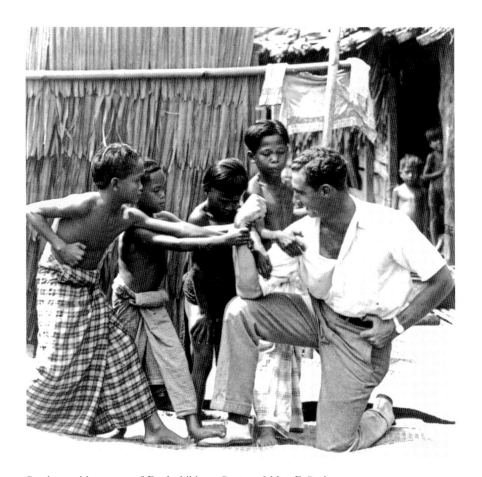

Stephens with a group of Dyak children. *Courtesy of Moye F. Stephens.*

Opposite: Letter from the Maharajah of Nepal thanking Richard Halliburton for the aerial show performed by Moye Stephens. *Courtesy of the Rhodes College Archives and Special Collections, Memphis, Tennessee.*

pool at the famous attraction, this time Halliburton hired another airplane to photograph the *Flying Carpet* with the Taj Mahal in the background. The pictures were sent through a syndicate to newspapers around the world with the caption, "In tales of old Asia, the Taj Mahal is usually associated with the story of the flying carpet, but here is the modern version. Richard Halliburton, American author and explorer, and Pilot Moye Stephens are touring the world flying over the famous temple at Delhi, India."[112]

Halliburton still couldn't resist "throwing on a little red paint" and making what he wrote about the adventure more exciting. This time, however, he had a witness in Stephens, and there were a few stories that were corrected during interviews in later years. For example, Halliburton wrote that they each "bought" a slave and then sold them back to the slave trader later at a loss. Stephens emphatically denied that and explained that the French officers with whom they spent much of their time would never have allowed such a thing. In another example, Halliburton wrote that when they departed the village of Dyak headhunters in Borneo, they were presented with twelve human heads, which Halliburton dramatically discarded one at a time as accidents continued to curse the two. As Stephens told biographer Michael Blankenship, "They wouldn't give us those heads. They're their prize possessions. And, of course, as far as putting ten or more heads in the airplane…boy, we loaded it down where we barely got off the water as it was. Things like that, Mike, in his estimation, livened the story up a bit."[113] Moye also shared with Blankenship his memory of a near disaster while capturing the first photo of Mount Everest from the air:

> *Richard wanted to go up and get a picture of Mt. Everest. Mt. Everest is 29,000 feet and the nominal ceiling of the Stearman is 16,000. By leaving out everything, our parachutes, tools, everything, just stripping it down and not even taking a full load of gas, I was able to waft it up to 18,000 by taking advantage of updrafts. Of course here was Everest another 11,000 feet above us. I had just turned off a ridge and turned sort of broadside so that Everest was right there, and Dick unfastened his belt and stood up in the cockpit to get a picture of this thing. Of course, with the increased drag of his body I was on the verge of a stall. Fortunately, I had turned away from the ridge and was headed down. When he stood up, the airplane lost its ceiling. It would have stalled if I hadn't nosed it down. I lost 1,000 feet or so. I reached up and batted him on the head when he did this, and he sat down. When we got back to Siliguri he said, "Well, tomorrow we'll go back and do that again. I'll get another picture of Mt. Everest." I said, "You and who else?"*[114]

One very nice surprise occurred during the journey while in Bushire on the Persian Gulf. Many times during their journey, the two men arrived at an airport to find they had just missed well-known German aviatrix Elly Beinhorn. Just a few weeks before they were in Timbuktu, Beinhorn experienced an engine failure on her way to West Africa and crash-landed in the Sahara. With the help of nomadic tribesmen, she joined a camel caravan to Timbuktu but had departed just before Halliburton and Stephens arrived. In Bushire, the three finally connected.

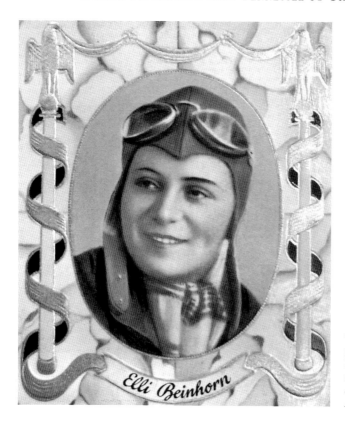

Collectible souvenir photo of Elly Beinhorn. *Courtesy of the Rhodes College Archives and Special Collections, Memphis, Tennessee.*

Only a few years earlier, Beinhorn had attended a lecture given by an aviator that ignited in her an interest in flying. With a small inheritance, and against the wishes of her parents, she moved to Berlin, where she learned to fly and began performing aerobatic stunts to supplement her income. She broke many distance records, and it was said her flying skills were only exceeded by her sense of style and femininity. It was during her own flight around the world that her plane began having mechanical difficulties, sixty miles north of Bushire. She was able to land and hitch a ride with a merchant who was on his way to the small town to purchase supplies. Moye Stephens's biographer, Barbara Schultz, wrote of their first meeting:

> *Elly stepped down from the truck, doing her best to shake off the dirt and present some semblance of propriety before entering. Moye, penning letters at the only writing desk in the guest lounge, looked up in amazement when Elly entered. Although he knew of her impending arrival from a telegram she sent to Bushire, he didn't expect such a lovely woman. Elly thought Moye must be*

the general manager until they introduced themselves. Several whiskies later, plans had been made to fly to Bandar Dilam in the morning and repair the Klemm which Elly referred to as "mein ehemann" (my husband).[115]

The three became instant friends, and Beinhorn referred to Halliburton and Stephens as "her papas." She took care of them by cutting their hair, darning their socks and bringing an elegant woman's touch to their adventures—while beating her male companions at swimming, driving and flying. They spent the next six weeks traveling together and exploring that part of world. With the introduction of the Victrola, theirs was the first generation that could easily transport recorded music from one place to another, and Halliburton and Beinhorn had both brought along a collection of records. At Beinhorn's suggestion, she and Halliburton exchanged their complete collections without either knowing what records the other had brought. Halliburton said she played her favorite, *St. Louis Blues*, seven times a day, while he and Stephens couldn't get enough of *Falling in Love Again*.[116] Love was in the air, and it's easy to imagine the three of them, in the dark of night with their two planes sitting far out in the desert, miles from anyone, with the only sound heard being Halliburton's Victrola playing Marlene Dietrich's recording of *Falling in Love Again*. Stephens, who saw in Beinhorn all the traits he was looking for in a wife, had fallen in love. He proposed, but Beinhorn was not yet ready to settle down and marry, nor did she want to move to the United States. She gently declined his proposal, and the two remained friendly. Both Halliburton and Stephens loved Beinhorn in their own way, so it was a meaningful moment for both as the two men stood and watched her airplane fly into the distance as she left them and headed for Australia. They picked up a letter from her in just a few days:

My Dear Papas,

Batavia was easy—only six hours—but it seemed like such a long time with no Flying Carpet *to keep me company. The world became very big again and very empty again after I left Singapore. What good am I without my two Papas? And what will you do without Elly? I'm sure you both will go to the dogs. But I'll play* St. Louis Blues *for you on my phonograph each day and you must play* Falling in Love Again *for me. I kiss you both on your sunburned noses—and will always stay your good child—*

Elly[117]

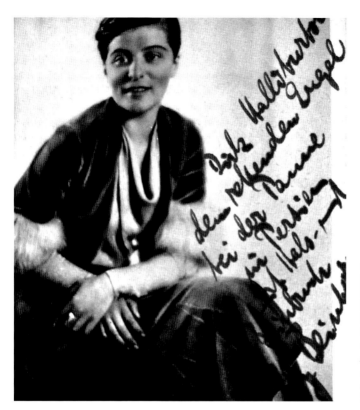

Autographed photo from Elly Beinhorn to Richard Halliburton. *Courtesy of the Rhodes College Archives and Special Collections, Memphis, Tennessee.*

In 1935, Elly Beinhorn's book, *Flying Girl*, was released, and Halliburton was happy to write the foreword for his friend. It included a description of that special time a few years earlier:

> *Just like everybody else, I fell in love with Elly on sight. She had the youngest, gayest, most buoyant personality I'd ever met. She infected everybody with her own happiness and her own vitality. Stephens and I hadn't laughed for weeks. Now we laughed at everything—especially at Elly and her funny German accent and broken-English curses when her engine wouldn't start…she thought nothing of spending an entire day in her overalls, with monkey wrench and oil can, dismembering engines. But when sundown came, she'd disappear for half and hour, and emerge in evening dress, looking so lovely, fragrant, so feminine, that Stephens and I were enchanted all over again each time.*[118]

Although Halliburton and Stephens got along well during their many months traveling together in what were often challenging circumstances, by

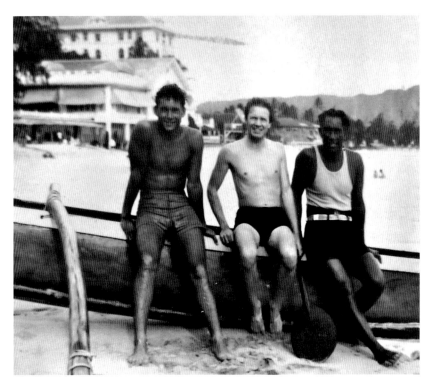

Duke Kahanamoku (right), Olympic medalist and father of modern surfing, and Richard Halliburton (center) in Honolulu, 1932. *Courtesy of the Rhodes College Archives and Special Collections, Memphis, Tennessee.*

Opposite: Promotional photo autographed for Halliburton by Duke Kahanamoku. The two met when Halliburton spent eight days in Honolulu after his *Flying Carpet* adventure. *Courtesy of the Rhodes College Archives and Special Collections, Memphis, Tennessee.*

the end of the journey, Halliburton began to grow weary of Stephens's lack of interest in anything other than flying. Stephens nursed Halliburton when he was sunburned to the point he needed medical attention, and Halliburton always made sure Stephens was treated as an equal among the important people they met along the way. They sometimes separated when they had free time in a city and did their own thing and then spent hours together in tight quarters when circumstances dictated.

On the way home, Halliburton and Stephens spent eight days in Honolulu, where Halliburton met Duke Kahanamoku, early beach volleyball player, five-time Olympic medalist in swimming and the father of modern surfing. Kahanamoku autographed a photo for Halliburton, who wrote to his

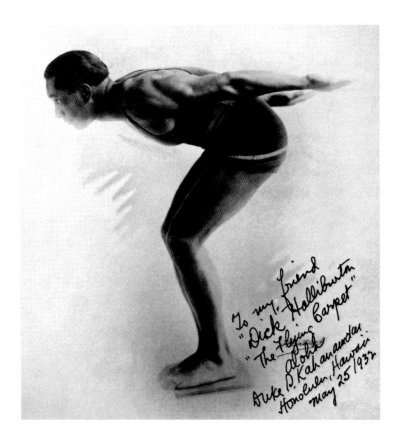

parents, "Eight days in Honolulu. Duke Kahanamoku, the famous Hawaiian swimmer, interested me."[119]

Richard Halliburton, Moye Stephens and the *Flying Carpet* finally made it home. At the end of his book, Halliburton wrote, "The *Flying Carpet* soared high into the sky of California, turned toward the south and arrived at last above familiar hills. Like a homing pigeon, the plane spiraled down to the airport from which, one morning some forty thousand miles before, we had set out to see the world."

Halliburton's fourth book hit the shelves in November 1932 with the following dedication: "To Moye W. Stephens, Jr. who piloted the *Flying Carpet*." The reviews from critics were more favorable than his previous books, with one writing, "If he keeps on like this, people who had been wishing he would make enough royalties to retire will wish instead that he would lose it all so he would have to keep writing about faraway places."[120] Little did they know that he no longer had it to lose.

CHAPTER 16

Lights, Camera, India

March 4, 1933
He's in the movies now! Having come face to face with most of the other great curiosities of the world, it was inevitable that Richard Halliburton sooner or later would get around to Hollywood. The man who scaled the Matterhorn, swam the Panama Canal, and lived with the head-hunters of the Borneo might pardonably have hesitated before attempting the fastness of movieland; but the dauntless Halliburton was never one to quail.
—Yorkshire Evening Press

Not everything Richard Halliburton touched turned to gold. On October 18, 1932, Halliburton wrote to his parents, "I've agreed to accept $10,000 for six weeks acting in a United Artist picture! I go to Hollywood on November third. I'm just as flabbergasted as you are."[121]

Brothers Walter and Fred Futter, who were producing the picture, were known as the "junk-men of filmdom" because they had compiled such a huge library of stock footage. Early in the development of motion pictures, they saw an opportunity and began buying negatives anywhere they could.[122] From bankrupt movie houses to freelancers who need a quick buck, they bought whatever they could get their hands on, regardless of the quality. Their company, Wafilms, also produced shorts for theatrical release that, like cartoons and newsreels, supplemented the main features. In 1930, Walter Futter directed, produced and edited a documentary called *Africa Speaks!*, which included footage shot during an expedition in the Serengeti. It was advertised as "the strangest romance ever filmed" and included new footage that was shot specifically for the film and then poorly edited into footage from the actual expedition. Narrated by travel writer Lowell Thomas, critics and audiences alike ate it up. *Photoplay* called it "an interesting travelogue with animal thrills, considerably dramatized," while the *New York Times* claimed it was "the most thrilling of travel pictures that have come to the screen."[123] Because of the success of *Africa Speaks!*, in December 1931, Walter Futter announced the development of six three-reel travelogues, including *Jade*, which would later become Halliburton's film *India Speaks!*

To create this new film, Futter used stock footage he owned of India, Tibet and the Himalayas, thrown in with a few new scenes featuring Halliburton and a "Kashmiri maiden" played by young actress Rosie Brown. Halliburton narrated the film just like Lowell Thomas had narrated *Africa Speaks!* It was a combination that couldn't fail. Except that it did.

Back in Memphis, Wesley Halliburton's intuition on the day his son flew away on the *Flying Carpet* proved correct—after Richard returned, things were never exactly the same again. The Halliburtons had purchased a lot on Court Avenue in Memphis and turned to Memphis architects George Mahan Jr. and Everett D. Woods to design the new Halliburton family home. A leader among Memphis architects at the time, Mahan designed numerous schools, banks and other public buildings in the city, including the Memphis Cotton Exchange and the King Cotton Hotel.

Halliburton wrote to his parents in late 1932, "Of course, our new house pleases me to pieces. It's going to be exactly what we want. A new house, a new book, a new movie, and all four of us in good health and high spirits—I think we have lots to be thankful for!"[124]

There was something else new that Halliburton didn't mention that would impact the relationship the elder Halliburtons had with their son. During his time exploring the world with Moye Stephens, he had been writing letters and sending much of the writing he was doing to his new secretary, Paul Mooney. From then on, whenever Halliburton referred to "our" book, his reference was to Mooney rather than to his parents, as it had been since his career had first begun.

Paul Mooney was born on November 4, 1904. His father, James Mooney, worked for the Smithsonian's Bureau of Ethnology for thirty-six years before he died in 1921. An expert in American Indian culture, at his memorial, he was hailed as a "patriotic citizen tolerant of all spiritual faiths."[125] After his father's death, Mooney became the head of the family at just sixteen. He quickly decided he wanted to be a writer, and after graduating from high

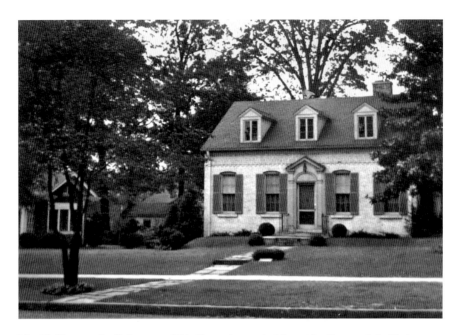

The Halliburton family home at 2275 Court Avenue in Memphis. *Courtesy of the Rhodes College Archives and Special Collections, Memphis, Tennessee.*

school, he secured a job as a cabin boy on a freighter and traveled from New York to Constantinople for an adventure very similar to Halliburton's early travels. He later dropped out of Catholic University of America in Washington, D.C., and moved to New York, where he wrote copy for advertising agencies. After spending some time in Paris, he returned to New York, where he continued to work as a freelance writer and photographer. After the stock market crash, Mooney followed the work to Hollywood, where he met Richard Halliburton. The two hit it off, and Halliburton quickly saw that Mooney had all the qualities he had been looking for in an assistant, chauffeur, secretary, editor—and love interest.

The two men communicated often while Halliburton was flying around the world, and in addition to sending a copy of his articles to his father, he began sending them to Mooney as well. After he and Mooney completed *The Flying Carpet*, he still struggled with financial problems, so he maintained an intense schedule of writing, speaking engagements, radio broadcasts and public appearances. *India Speaks!* finally offered him the opportunity to make the transition into the lucrative movie business. As he once wrote to his parents, "The money thrown around out here appalls me. People of the

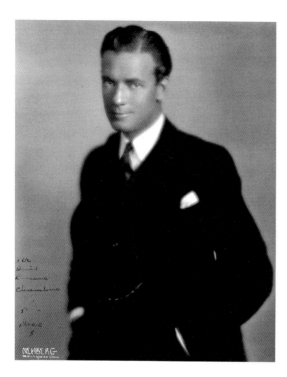

Promotional photograph from the studio of Philip Newberg of Hollywood. The photo is autographed by Halliburton to David Laurance Chambers of Bobbs-Merrill. *Courtesy of The Lilly Library, Indiana University.*

commonest, stupidest type get $5,000, $7,000, $10,000 a week. Any actor or director or writer receiving less than $1,000 feels ready to join a revolution. At the same time other people are starving by the thousands."[126]

The concern he expressed to his conservative parents for those who were starving didn't keep him from enjoying Hollywood and the chance to become an equal with the superstars of the day. In a movie magazine interview, arranged to promote his film, he cleverly positioned himself as just another one of the Hollywood gang:

> *"Meeting Mary Pickford…was one of my happiest experiences,"* he relates. *"Just as exciting as when I met the Queen of Persia or the Empress of China. Not because Mary is a movie star, but because she's a woman with a great mind, heart and character. Charlie Chaplin delighted me with his easy friendliness. We had met before in Singapore, on our respective trips around the world, he by steamer and I by airplane. His arrival in Singapore caused the biggest excitement of the year. At a party at Gary Cooper's the other night, Charlie, Doug Fairbanks and I had a three-sided discussion about our voyages and adventures.*[127]

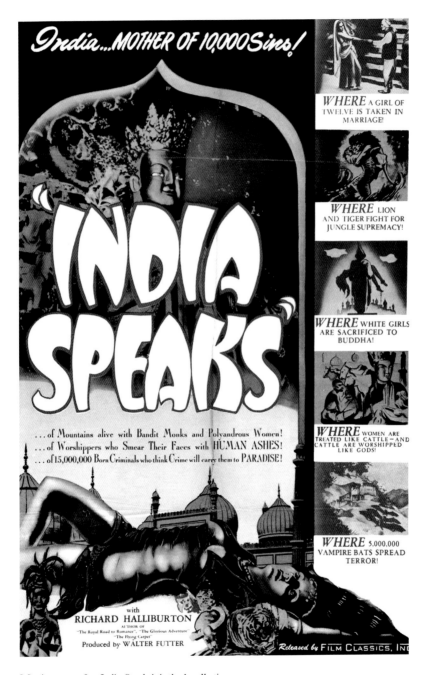

Movie poster for *India Speaks! Author's collection.*

The movie premiered at the New Roxy Theater in New York in May 1933, and Halliburton added movie promotional appearances to his list of nonstop activities that included lectures, book signings, newspaper interviews and radio shows. It's possible his parents went to see *India Speaks!* at the Lowes State Theater on Main Street in Memphis. Ads for the showing of the movie in his hometown featured the headline "Richard Halliburton, Memphis' Own Famous Son, Author of Many Best Sellers, Reveals Secrets of 1,000 Years!" And if that didn't do enough to sell tickets, the ad also included the tease "WHERE STRANGE GODS LOOK DOWN UNASHAMED ON HUMAN ORGIES!"

The movie opened to a lukewarm reception and quickly disappeared. It was time for Halliburton to return to writing. Although reviews of *The Flying Carpet* were mixed and it was not selling as well as his previous books, Chambers was anxious to get a new one in the pipeline. The Depression was hitting the publishing business especially hard, as many customers no longer had the money to spend on unnecessary items like books when they were now struggling just to get food on the table. Halliburton was a proven commodity and a recognized brand on which Bobbs-Merrill knew it could count.

It was time for a new adventure.

CHAPTER 17

Pinnacle of Success

August 19, 1935
The young man gritted his teeth and ran his fingers thru his reddish blonde hair as he sat on a green porch swing at his home, 2275 Court…"That's like the story about the dog biting my elephant in Italy. Let me tell you what happened." Mr. Halliburton stretched out farther on the green swing in the morning sunlight. He used his hands in excessive gestures as he became more engrossed in his tale.
—Memphis Press-Scimitar

By 1935, Richard Halliburton was counted among the most well-known writers in the nation. A deal with the Bell Newspaper Syndicate put full-page spreads of his articles in fifty newspapers around the country every Sunday for a year. He got to pick where he went and the topics that would be included in each article. When compiled, the articles became his fifth book for Bobbs-Merrill, *Seven League Boots*, which he dedicated to Mary Hutchison.

As he wrote in the introduction, "My only orders were to move fast, visit strange places, try to meet whomever I thought interesting and important—and to start at once."[128] The stories took him from Havana, Haiti and Santo Domingo to France, Germany, Russia and the Middle East. Along the way, he fished with the Seri Indians, met the oldest man in the world, interviewed Vladimir Lenin's widow and touched the bones of Christopher Columbus. Two other stories in particular that came out of this series captured the imagination and attention not just of his fans in the United States but also of readers around the world. And these two stories couldn't have been more different.

Hannibal, an ancient military commander, performed one of the most celebrated military moves in ancient history when, around 220 BC, it's said he assembled thirty to forty thousand men and around forty elephants and marched from Iberia over the Pyrenees and the Alps into northern Italy. Following the same path intrigued Halliburton, but he first needed to find an elephant. After several didn't work out for a variety of reasons, a small zoo in a children's park in Paris had an elephant that Halliburton thought would work well. In October 1934, Elysabethe Dalrymple, or "Dally," as Halliburton called his new elephant comrade, joined him to begin the trip from Paris. She made it as far as the street outside the zoo. Apparently, Dally wasn't familiar with the noisy traffic on the streets of Paris, and she became so terrified that she bolted and ran for a half mile before she could be caught. Halliburton decided to go to Berlin to secure another elephant that was available, but when he arrived, he discovered she was pregnant and unable to travel. It was now too late to get an elephant ready before the Great St. Bernard Pass closed due to the winter snow. His "crossing the Alps on an elephant" adventure would have to wait.

While in Berlin trying to rent an elephant, Halliburton stumbled upon what would become for many one of his most fascinating stories and what every writer hopes for—the scoop of a lifetime. He wrote to his parents from Germany, "Uniforms are everywhere. The older people seem very cool about Hitler, but the kids here are all maniacs on the subject—and they will be in command in a few years."[129] After several weeks in Berlin, Halliburton, who valued his freedom to do as he pleased above all else, had already had enough. "For one used to, and requiring personal freedom to travel, to read, to enjoy the fine things that make life worth living, Russia is a hateful, tyrannical prison cell."[130]

According to Halliburton biographer Jonathan Root's account, Halliburton was staying at the Hotel Metropole, which was the gathering place for foreign correspondents. They showed him the ropes for gathering news in Russia, and William Stoneman of the *Chicago Daily News* even gave him a tip that would lead to the interview that all the correspondents wanted—with the man in charge of the mass murder of Nicholas II, the last emperor of Russia; his wife, Alexandra Feodorovna; his son, Alexei; and his four daughters—Olga, Tatiana, Maria and Anastasia. The Romanov Dynasty had ruled Russia since 1613 but ended on March 15, 1917, when Nicholas II, who had ruled for twenty-three years, was brought down when mutinous soldiers from his own army joined forces with Russian revolutionaries. As the economy and military collapsed around them, the family and some of their faithful servants were held captive and, in July 1918, gathered in a room and viciously executed. Seventeen years later, Richard Halliburton was on a train on the Trans-Siberian Railway headed from Moscow to Sverdlovsk, where one of the alleged assassins, Peter Zacharovitch Ermakov, was said to be living. Halliburton had hired Stoneman's interpreter, who he later said turned out to be a spy. When Halliburton arrived at the home of Ermakov, the latter was coughing and spitting up blood. He was supposedly dying of throat cancer and was suddenly ready to give Halliburton his deathbed confession. Ermakov shared in graphic detail how he and two others stood in the doorway of the room in which the Romanoffs waited, read their death sentence and then killed them all for their crimes against the Russian people. Anastasia, who was rumored for years to have escaped, was "clubbed to death with rifle butts." According to Ermakov, they then built a funeral pyre, "piled the bodies on two layers deep" and, using sulfuric acid and gasoline, burned them continually until there was nothing left but ashes. Ermakov then personally scattered the ashes out across a field, where any remaining evidence would have been destroyed by the next day's rain. He added, "So if anybody says he has seen a Romanoff, or a piece of a dead one—tell him about the ashes—and the wind—and the rain."[131]

You can sense Halliburton's excitement over the story in a letter written to his parents shortly afterward:

> *The Sverdlovsk expedition was a grand and glorious success, beyond my wildest hopes. The man who murdered the Czar and all his family, the actual assassin who was jailor, executioner, undertaker, cremator, has kept silent for seventeen years. I got him on his sick bed, and heard his story poured out—unguarded, complete and terrifically vivid. I happened by this good break to be his confessor. He's never spoken to any other person. I'm still a little weak over the melodramatics of the thing. This interview should insure* [sic] *the success of our book. It was history told me. The story is so tremendous I'm writing it for* Liberty *or* Cosmopolitan.[132]

The Bell Syndicate distributed the story in four installments. Some believed Ermakov was lying, while others believed it was Halliburton who was making up the story. According to Jonathan Root, Stoneman, the reporter who initially shared the tip, accused Halliburton of being "a storyteller posing as a journalist." It wasn't the first time he had heard that accusation, and it wouldn't be the last.

It was midsummer 1935, and Halliburton had nearly completed his fifty stories. He refused to let the elephant be the one that got away. He arrived

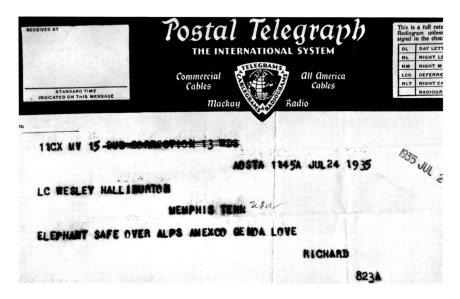

A July 1935 telegram Halliburton sent his father letting him know Dally had made it over the Alps. *Courtesy of the Rhodes College Archives and Special Collections, Memphis, Tennessee.*

in Paris and began a month of preparations for an elephant ride across the Alps to Rome. Since their failed first attempt, Dally had learned to follow a truck down the street and was less afraid of traffic. As they began their well-publicized adventure, Dally and Halliburton were followed by hundreds of spectators, including many children who were seeing their very first elephant. On their way out of town, they stopped at the local children's hospital, where Halliburton dismounted and gave Dally room to play her harmonica for the young patients who had gathered in the courtyard. Halliburton later told a *Memphis Press-Scimitar* reporter that there were seven movie cameras, twenty news photographers and many of the large European newspapers sent journalists along to cover the journey. After three days of walking, the altitude began to cause Dally to struggle, so the pace slowed until they finally reached the gates of the St. Bernard Monastery, where more than two thousand area residents, fifteen monks, more than a dozen St. Bernard dogs and scores of journalists and photographers were there to greet them. During the advance preparations, Halliburton had secured an appropriate place for Dally to spend the night—the monks moved their truck out of their garage and covered the floor in hay.

Unfortunately, Halliburton and Dally didn't make it much farther. After leaving the monastery, they came upon an Italian regiment doing maneuvers, and Dally was startled into another mad dash—but this time she ran nearly a mile before she was finally found. Later, the truck they were following was damaged in a traffic accident, and finally, Dally's feet began to become too sore to continue. She was put in a freight car loaded with hay and sent back to the Paris zoo.

In the grainy, black-and-white footage that exists from that stunt, Halliburton clearly relished the attention he and his elephant were receiving, and the crowds were electrified by their proximity to both a famous American writer and a real live elephant. Journalists, especially in Europe, couldn't get enough of the story, and photographs, drawings, cartoons and detailed updates appeared in newspapers every day. Dally wasn't the *Spirit of St. Louis*, but in Switzerland and France, at least for a little while, Halliburton was even more famous than Charles Lindbergh.

Halliburton's adventure with the elephant was the last of the syndicated articles distributed by Bell and the last chapter in *Seven League Boots*. Before leaving Paris, he went to the zoo to bid farewell to Dally and to present her with a new, extra-large harmonica. In the last paragraph of his book, Halliburton wrote, "And as I walked away, with a lump in my throat, I still heard fading behind me the whine of the harmonica, and I felt sure that though she may have been foot-sore and travel-weary, Elysabethe Dalrymple, besides being at that moment the most famous elephant in the world, was the happiest."[133]

CHAPTER 18

Hangover House

January 20, 1957
The ghost of Richard Halliburton, some folks believe, still prowls that monolithic monument to the late adventurer—Hangover House. Strange "flashing lights" have been reported in the cavernous concrete and steel structure which climbs skyward from a ridge 500 feet over the Pacific.
—Cedar Rapids Gazette

On the train—October 15, 1936

Mother dear:

This is a letter just for you. Sometimes I want to love you specially and apart from Dad and discuss things that concern only you and me. We're not a very demonstrative family, and so I have to write to you what I sometimes fail to show and say…I wanted to tell you when I was home about the rumor of my new house in California. You showed antagonism to the idea before I could tell you about it, and I hesitated to disturb our all-too-few days of happiness together…I first saw Laguna then fell in love with it. Sometime after, during the worst of the depression, I was riding horseback one day two miles south of the town on the beach. I looked up and saw a ridge rising broadside 800 feet from the shore. I rode up it to the summit of the ridge to get the view…the view enchanted me and every time I saw it I had a vision of a house on this spectacular ridge. I talked about it for months…the designing of this house has been enormous fun—a special *house for a special place…the house will be finished some time next year. I will not see it until late April when my tour takes me west. I am calling it Hangover House, because it overhangs the precipice. If I had a million dollars, I wouldn't change one inch of it. When it's finished I shall prevail upon you and Dad to visit me, and when you see it, you too will fall in love with it and be happy with me that I own it.*[134]

Before Hangover House was complete, it would stretch to the breaking point Richard Halliburton's nerves, his relationships and his bank account. Upon completion, the final cost had soared to more than three times the original estimate. When Halliburton's friend and Hangover House architect, William Alexander, mentioned someone he knew was interested in buying it, Halliburton responded, "The only customer that will ever be willing to take Hangover off my hands will be Orange County, for taxes."[135]

The Laguna Beach Halliburton first visited, and with which he fell in love almost immediately, was home to hundreds of artists, musicians, writers, poets, actors and creative minds from all areas of the arts. The seeds of its creativity had been planted around 1906, when Norman St. Clair, an English watercolor artist and architect who was living in Pasadena, California, began taking the stagecoach to Laguna Beach and found the natural sunlight to have a unique quality that was especially effective for painting outdoors. St. Clair's artwork included the ocean, surf, canyons and hills around the area, and after a one-man show in which his watercolors were a huge success, other artists began visiting the area and creating their own art.

Drawn to the light and natural beauty of the area, artists like William Wendt, Anna Althea Hills and Edgar and Elsie Palmer Payne made Laguna Beach their home. In 1918, they joined many other artists and formed the Laguna Beach Art Association, and what would become a celebrated artist colony was born. In 1926, their section of the Pacific Coast Highway was completed, and Laguna Beach was instantly linked with Hollywood. Once the movie industry discovered the effect the area's natural sunlight had on film, it became the location for many silent movies, including *Captain Blood*, *Robinson Crusoe* and *Robin Hood*. Many of Halliburton's Hollywood friends like Charlie Chaplin, Mary Pickford, Douglass Fairbanks Jr. and Rudolph Valentino built second homes in the area, and beating Halliburton as the first writer in town, John Steinbeck wrote *Tortilla Flat* in 1935 while living there. Although not the first, Halliburton certainly became the most famous writer in town at the time. The success and nationwide distribution of his newspaper and magazine articles, his books on the bestseller lists and the hundreds of thousands who had heard him lecture in person had made him a literary superstar. He could demand the highest possible fees for his lectures and, with Paul Mooney's assistance, was able to churn out more articles than ever before. He and Chambers had decided the next book should be for children, and once he finished gathering stories and photos, they decided there was enough content for two volumes. The first would focus on the Western, or Occidental, part of the world and the other on the Eastern, or Oriental, part.

Paul Mooney played a crucial role during this time, functioning as secretary, ghostwriter and editor, and was still a significant part of Halliburton's small, intimate social circle. Although the two were obviously together romantically, it appears they were never exclusive, as both spent time with other men and were apart from each other as much as they were together. Mooney was especially close to architect William Alexander Levy (the "Levy" was later dropped from his name). Born in Brooklyn in 1909 to Russian-Jewish immigrant parents, Alexander was the youngest of fifteen siblings. The two met in 1930 when both were New York University students and attended a class taught by author Thomas Wolfe. Mooney spent the early years of the depression working odd jobs to get himself through college, eventually becoming a teaching assistant at NYU, where he studied at the School of Architecture. His greatest influence came firsthand from pioneers of modern architecture Frank Lloyd Wright and Le Corbusier.

In 1936, Halliburton contacted the young architect in New York and finally commissioned the design of the house of which he had long dreamed. Unfortunately, the construction became more of a nightmare for all three men. Initially, all went well, and Mooney and Alexander moved into a bungalow on the beach that was close to the site to supervise the construction. Halliburton gave orders and directed from the road, where he was speaking and writing in order to make more money to spend on the house. As a testimony to the close nature of their relationship, Hangover House was being built with three bedrooms: one for Halliburton, one for Mooney and one for Alexander. The entire structure was built from poured concrete and perched over the side of a cliff that was five hundred feet above the ocean below. For his first solo project of significance, Alexander was greatly influenced by both the International Style of architecture and his appreciation of Frank Lloyd Wright. As explained by Anthony Denzer in an article for the *Southern California Quarterly*:

> *Alexander would have been familiar with the 1932 "Modern Architecture" exhibition at MOMA, which was undoubtedly discussed at NYU, and*

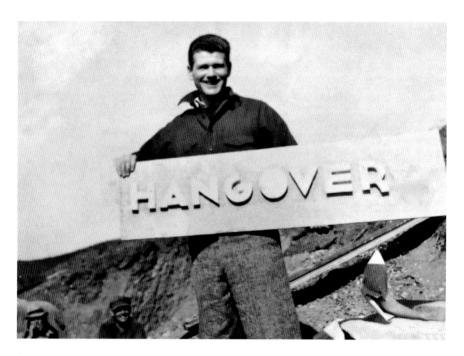

Paul Mooney with the Hangover House sign, 1937. *Courtesy of the Michael E. Blankenship Collection of the Halliburton Archives, Rhodes College.*

> *thus with the aesthetic principles of the International Style—abstract cubic volumes, asymmetric balance, flat roofs, ribbon windows and thin steel railings—all of which he used in the Halliburton House. But the house also exhibits Alexander's first-hand exposure to Wright's principles. The structure's overhangs and deep shadows were characteristic of Wright, not of the tightly wrapped International Style. The plan, like so many Wright houses, followed an asymmetric cruciform pattern, with the hearth located as a focal point near the cross-axes. Moreover, Alexander built small variations in the level floor surface, which created a hierarchy of spaces within a relatively simple and open floor plan, and the complex entry sequence used expanding and contracting spaces to amplify the sense of transition and shelter.*[136]

The materials were carried up to the ridge by the laborers Mooney and Alexander had hired, many of whom were unskilled transients looking for work during the depression. To make matters even more difficult, there was a shortage of materials because of the reconstruction that was taking place in the area after an earthquake in San Francisco. The cost of the construction became much more than anticipated, and the relationship between Alexander and Halliburton soured to the point that Alexander was planning to walk away from the project when it was only halfway completed. Halliburton knew it would be impossible to finish the house without him, and he charmed Alexander into staying on the job. The original estimate for building Hangover House was $10,000, but the final cost was more than $36,000. Mooney managed the finances and "supervised" but spent much of his time drinking, smoking cigarettes and taking photographs of the construction.

Despite the cost overruns and drama the construction was causing, Halliburton continued to sing its praises to his parents. In a letter on April 18, 1937, he wrote, "I got to Laguna yesterday afternoon and rushed to the house. I can't say in words how amazing it is. Pictures just don't give a small part of its charm and beauty. It doesn't sit. It flies."[137]

Halliburton, who had already put a little more distance between him and his parents, continued to spend less time with them once construction began on Hangover House. Although he had certainly spent much time away from his parents, once Hangover House was complete, their home would no longer be his home. They were greatly concerned, and Wesley Halliburton told his son that he feared he was becoming morose and cynical and was isolating himself from others. He also expressed concern for his son's spiritual life. After reassuring his father that he had no plans to become a hermit, Halliburton answered, "Please don't be distressed because I am the way I am. Just be grateful that I am so much happier than most people and trying to go on an up-climbing curve, rather than marking time with those who have come from the regulation mold."[138] In another letter, he wrote:

> I've read and reread Dad's letter repeatedly. I agree with him that once I'm on my mountain-top house I'll be able to adjust my life onto a calmer plane and grow in spirit rather than in mileage. If I never get nearer the Eternal in that house, then it's not in me. I never saw a house so far away from man and so close to God. The peace and serenity of that canyon is enough in itself to make one relax and dream.[139]

During construction, the house became a curiosity among locals, and the site was often crowded with visitors who came to check out the unusual structure. Ayn Rand, celebrated novelist and playwright, visited the house, and Alexander later suggested the descriptions of Enright House in Rand's best-selling novel *The Fountainhead* were inspired by her visit. It's likely that

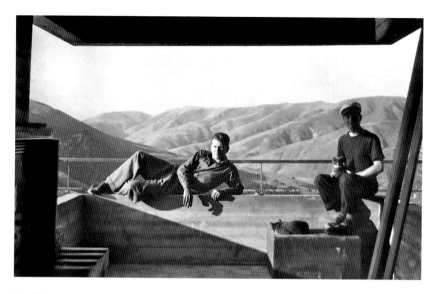

Paul Mooney and William Alexander at the Hangover House construction site, 1937.
Courtesy of the Michael E. Blankenship Collection of the Halliburton Archives, Rhodes College.

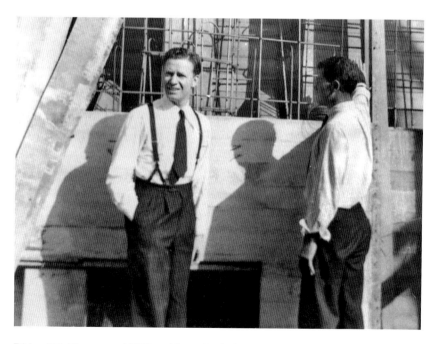

Richard Halliburton and William Alexander during construction of Hangover House, 1937. *Courtesy of the Michael E. Blankenship Collection of the Halliburton Archives, Rhodes College.*

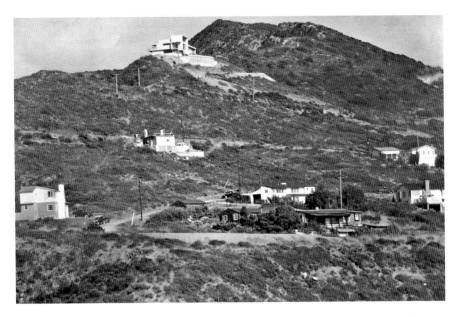

Area surrounding the Hangover House construction site, 1937. *Courtesy of the Michael E. Blankenship Collection of the Halliburton Archives, Rhodes College.*

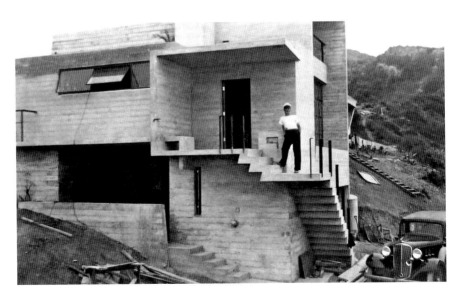

William Alexander at the Hangover House construction site, 1937. *Courtesy of the Michael E. Blankenship Collection of the Halliburton Archives, Rhodes College.*

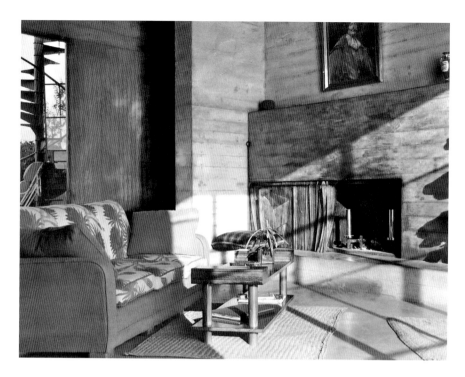

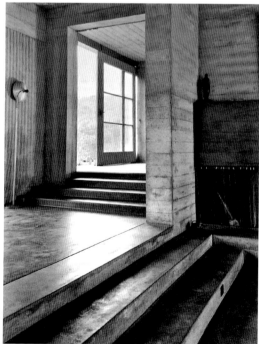

Above: Hangover House living room, 1937. *Courtesy of the Michael E. Blankenship Collection of the Halliburton Archives, Rhodes College.*

Left: Hangover House hallway, 1937. *Courtesy of the Michael E. Blankenship Collection of the Halliburton Archives, Rhodes College.*

Rand had met Alexander back in New York when the two were working together at the same architectural firm. While the house was under construction, she was living nearby in Hollywood.[140]

Hangover House also included features that were new or even unheard of at the time. Early visitors were impressed with the custom sliding doors, a steel spiral staircase, one of the very first garbage disposals and even a dumbwaiter that connected all three floors.

On August 16, 1937, fifteen months after construction began, Halliburton spent the first night in his new home. He wrote, "It's completely empty, but beautiful and satisfying even so."[141] The Princeton alumni magazine noted, "Dick Halliburton is getting to be like any other mortal. He's built him a home. Next thing we'll hear is that he's married and bragging about his youngsters like everyone else."

Just like they did with his books, the national media critiqued Halliburton's new home. From the *New York Times* to *Look* magazine and the *Architectural Record*, the reviews were all positive. His new home was a hit, and he was certainly pleased others thought as much of Hangover House as he did. The landscaping was heralded as "spectacular," and the house was referred to as a "modern mansion." Architectural critic Sidney Lawrence wrote, "Space in the hands of Alexander has become a symbol of the world of action, change, adventure."[142]

After completion of the house, the three had certainly had enough of one another. Alexander quickly returned to New York, while Mooney planned to head south. Richard Halliburton had spent way more money on Hangover House than he ever intended. Once again, he was desperately in need of funds, so it was time for another adventure. Sadly, this would be his last.

CHAPTER 19

The Sea Dragon

September 27, 1938
We suggest a pair of Seven League boots for Mrs. Wesley Halliburton. She needs them! Back from Europe only three days, she answered the wire of her famous author-son, Richard, and went traipsing off to California...Mrs. Halliburton attended a party for Tallulah Bankhead and another given for Richard...Mrs. Halliburton saw Richard set sail for China Friday on the President Coolidge. He has gone in search of a Chinese junk, which he plans to anchor off Treasure Island where the exposition will be held.
—Memphis Press-Scimitar

Laurance Chambers finally received a reply from his urgent wire to Indiana congressman Louis Ludlow, and the news about Halliburton's missing junk was hopeful. Congressman Ludlow wrote that he had checked with navigation experts, and they believed the Chinese junk on which Halliburton and thirteen crewmen were sailing was likely safe and that their radio was just out of service. As Chambers told reporters, his concern was not only as the head of the publishing house that published Halliburton's books but also as a close, personal friend. After reading that Senator Kenneth McKellar of Tennessee had been asked by Wesley Halliburton to petition the government for assistance in locating the junk, Chambers thought a telegram to his own Washington representative couldn't hurt. Knowing Halliburton, Chambers was asked by reporters if this was another stunt by the adventure writer to sell more books. He replied, "He is too

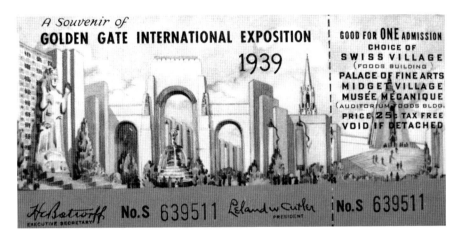

Ticket for the 1939 Golden Gate International Exposition. *Courtesy of the Rhodes College Archives and Special Collections, Memphis, Tennessee.*

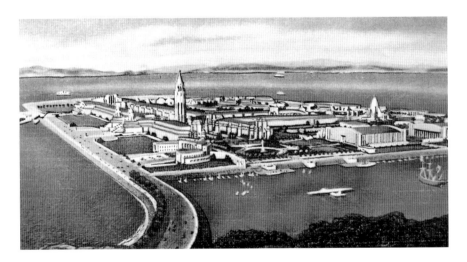

Artist's rendering of Treasure Island at the exposition. Note what appears to be the *Sea Dragon* in the lower right corner. *Courtesy of the Rhodes College Archives and Special Collections, Memphis, Tennessee.*

affectionate and devoted a son to cause his parents such distress and worry. Not only that, but many of the members of the crew of the *Sea Dragon* were American college boys whom he had taken along just because they wanted to go. The families of these men are just as concerned as Halliburton's family."[143] But even as the words were tumbling out of his mouth, he had to be remembering his feelings years earlier when he received word Halliburton had drowned while attempting to swim the Hellespont. That time, it was days before Halliburton let Chambers know it was all a publicity stunt to sell books, so there's no doubt he said a silent prayer that this would turn out the same—and boy would he let Halliburton have it if it did.

This whole fiasco started out as a simple promotion for a fair. The Golden Gate International Exposition, held in 1939 at San Francisco's Treasure Island, was an opportunity to build the region's morale, create new jobs and increase the number of tourists who visited the area by capitalizing on the recent openings of the Golden Gate and Oakland Bay Bridges. Additionally, the organizers wanted to position the area as a gateway to Latin America and the hub of the Pan-Asian world. The look of the exposition was an eclectic combination of Myan, Cambodian, Cubist and Art Deco styles, and in promotional materials the architecture was described as "a new 'Pacific' style that has been devised to exalt the visitor spiritually into a 'Never-Never Land' where romance is in the air."[144] Few celebrities better embodied the concepts of modern style, world travel and romance-filled air than Richard Halliburton.

While the bridges were being constructed, Halliburton wanted to check them out for a story he was writing for his *Book of Marvels*. Recognizing a great public relations opportunity when he saw one, Walter Swanson, vice-president of the San Francisco Convention and Tourist Bureau, made the arrangements for the visit to each bridge and then made certain there were plenty of reporters there to cover Halliburton's private tour. As they chatted, Swanson realized Halliburton was just the man they had been looking for to help provide an exciting kick-off event for the upcoming exposition. Swanson proposed a journey across the Pacific timed so that Halliburton would arrive dramatically during the opening-night festivities to great fanfare and celebration. Swanson shared his idea with others on the promotional team, including Clyde Vandeburg, director of publicity and promotion, and Art Linkletter, who was handling the radio promotions for the exposition. Linkletter shared his memories of Halliburton in his 1960 autobiography, *Confessions of a Happy Man*:

> I remember sitting in Clyde Vandeburg's office with Richard Halliburton, the handsome and romantic young man whose unique travel books were best sellers. Opening ceremonies were always a problem…and we thought we had a winner in Halliburton. The plan was to have him go to China, buy a large and colorful junk and sail it across the Pacific. He was certain he

could arrive outside the Golden Gate on opening day and his triumphant entry—up to that time no man had attempted such a risky feat—would officially launch the fair. We would meet him offshore and get an exclusive report on the trip for a network show.

"*You have no doubts about this trip?*" *Vandeburg asked.*

"*None at all,*" *Halliburton said.*

I can still see him sitting there—lean, bronzed by the sun, impeccably groomed and tailored. The starched cuffs of his shirt protruded two inches from the sleeves and there was a silk handkerchief tucked into one cuff.[145]

Both the world around Richard Halliburton and the popular culture that had made him famous were rapidly changing and evolving as both he and the century were approaching forty. Although the *Book of Marvels* had been released to positive reviews, and he still had a strong following, the audiences in his lectures had decreased steadily in size. If Americans sat in a theater in 1937, it was likely to watch a movie rather than a lecture. Suddenly, Tyrone Power, Clark Gable and Spencer Tracy were doing the same things Halliburton had been lecturing about, and moviegoers could watch it happen right before their very eyes. Of course, now they could also sit at home and listen to the radio. Approximately 26 million families owned at least one radio, and they now spent an average of five hours a day listening to news, music and their favorite shows.[146] Now, instead of having to drive to a theater or school auditorium to hear a lecture about travel to another country, they could stay at home and listen to programs like *The Edgar Bergen and Charlie McCarthy Show*, *Burns and Allen* and *Fibber McGee and Molly*. Suddenly, the superstars of the day were Bob Hope, Fred Allen and Jack Benny.

Just a few years earlier, a Richard Halliburton lecture in Central Texas would've been filled to capacity. But at an appearance at Baylor University in 1938, the good seats—the ones set up in the orchestra section—were less than half filled. Fifteen-year-old R.C. Phelan had gone to great lengths to be in the audience that night to hear his favorite author. He wrote, "[Halliburton was] brown-haired and nearly handsome, dressed in a dark suit. He came to the middle of the stage, looked up at the students in the balcony, and called, 'Would you people like to come downstairs? There are plenty of seats here.'"[147] Little did he know that this would be a big infraction at Baylor because the organizer felt it was unfair to those who had paid extra for the good seats. A post-lecture reception was angrily canceled, which freed Halliburton up to invite his young fan to have dinner. During their time together that evening, Halliburton shared advice with

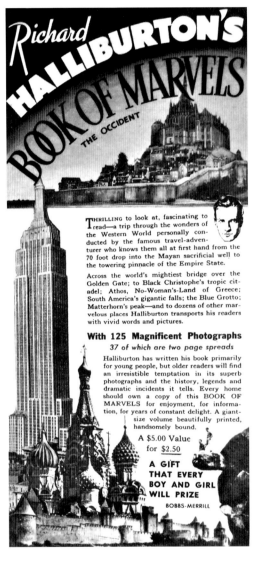

Print advertisement for *Richard Halliburton's Book of Marvels: The Occident. Courtesy of the Rhodes College Archives and Special Collections, Memphis, Tennessee.*

Phelan. He stressed, "You have to dramatize things a bit to make them more interesting."[148] A little of the Halliburton magic must have rubbed off that night, as R.C. Phelan later became a successful newspaper reporter, English professor and a magazine writer for publications like *Vogue*, the *Saturday Evening Post*, *Redbook* and many others.

With lecture attendances dwindling and his books no longer selling as well as he would have liked, Halliburton knew it was time for a change. Once he made the money he needed from this journey across the Pacific, he could return to Laguna Beach, spend more time at Hangover House and finally write a serious book on a topic like Rupert Brooke. But first he had to get the next adventure underway, and for that he needed cash—and lots of it.

Getting funding secured for this adventure would end up being harder than Halliburton ever anticipated. First, the initial investors, four wealthy Chinese merchants, backed out because they were afraid the junk would never be allowed to leave China during the war with Japan. By 1938, tens of thousands of Chinese civilians had been killed by the Japanese, and with the fall of Nanking in December 1937, Japanese soldiers had embarked on a six-week orgy of murder, rape, mutilation and torture. China was not an easy place in which to do business in 1938.

Turning to the United States, Halliburton found few willing to take a chance and invest in such an expedition. Even his own millionaire cousin, Erle Halliburton, refused to give him any money—but a few others, including Erle Halliburton's wife and two of his daughters, invested. Erle Halliburton's daughter Zola helped him get most of the money he needed when she connected Halliburton with John Potter and Robert Chase, two young men from wealthy families who were anxious for an adventure. The previous year, the two had been vacationing in Bermuda and had run into Zola Halliburton, who knew Potter from school. The two boys, bored and looking for adventure, decided on a whim to build a skiff and sail it back to New York. The idea was ill conceived at best, and they had to be towed back to Bermuda by the Coast Guard. Zola Halliburton joked that if they were that ready for an adventure, she should introduce them to her cousin Richard. She later shared the story with her cousin, and Halliburton wrote Potter and offered the experience of sailing from Hong Kong to San Francisco on a junk. Of course, anyone who wanted to come along would have to financially invest in the expedition. The young men convinced their families to invest and invited several other wealthy friends to join them.

The Bell Syndicate paid Halliburton for a series of articles, and he even crossed over from the editorial side of the newspaper business to the advertising side and negotiated a sponsorship with the *San Francisco News*. He would return to San Francisco and lecture at schools throughout California to promote the newspaper. The plan for generating revenue also included rides on the junk for one dollar per passenger and the sale of souvenirs during the exposition. Eventually, he raised almost all the money needed to fund the purchase of a junk in Hong Kong and the supplies needed to get a crew across the Pacific. In order to raise the final $4,000, he mortgaged Hangover House. Now, if this expedition failed, he would lose the home he had worked so hard to build. Everything was now at stake.

On September 23, 1938, Halliburton and Captain John Welch boarded the *President Coolidge* in San Francisco and headed for Hong Kong. Hesitant and not at all looking forward to the journey, Paul Mooney had been persuaded to join the expedition and was along for the ride as well. As the three men began the initial leg of the journey, Halliburton wrote his first article for the Bell Syndicate, which included his vision for the launching of the great ship. He wrote, "The name? I chose that long ago—the *Sea Dragon*.

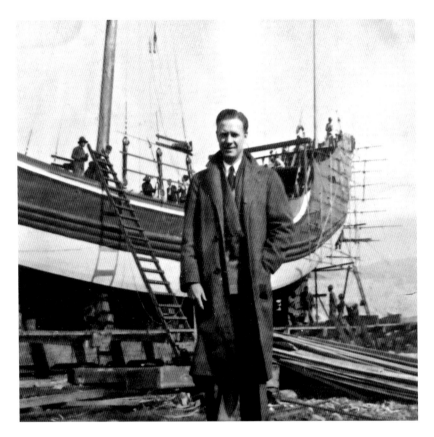

Richard Halliburton posing in front of the *Sea Dragon* on December 29, 1938. Photo taken by Dr. and Mrs. J.M. Lapp, missionaries Halliburton had written about in his first book in a chapter titled "Tiger Tales." *Courtesy of the Rhodes College Archives and Special Collections, Memphis, Tennessee.*

On the day of launching, the prettiest Chinese girl whom I can find will break a bottle of rice wine on the *Sea Dragon*'s nose. And as the junk slides down the ways we'll all beat gongs and shoot off firecrackers, in proper Chinese fashion, to drive away the demons of storm and shipwreck."[149]

Almost immediately, things didn't go as planned. Once word spread down the China coast that a wealthy American was looking to buy a junk, the prices suddenly tripled. It eventually became clear that they were not going to be able to find a junk they could afford, so they moved on to the next best thing. They would have to build one. A shipbuilder was recommended, and Halliburton went to meet with him in person. Of the meeting, he wrote, "Mr. Fat Kau welcomed us graciously. We were clearly a group of foreign

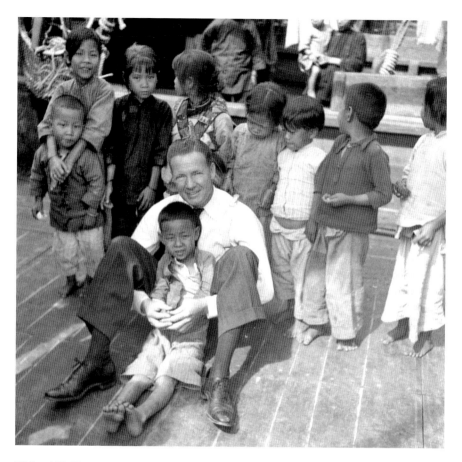

Richard Halliburton with a group of children from an orphanage in Hong Kong. *Courtesy of the Michael M. Blankenship Collection of the Halliburton Archives, Rhodes College.*

idiots…wanting to build a junk and name it the *Sea Dragon* and sail it to San Francisco, 9,000 miles away. But we were cash customers, so the generous man agreed, finally to accept only twice what we offered…If anyone wishes to be driven rapidly and violently insane, and doesn't know how to go about it, let me make a suggestion: Try building a Chinese junk in a Chinese shipyard, during a war with Japan."[150]

Halliburton's friend and fellow author and journalist Gordon Sinclair was in Hong Kong as a war correspondent and was with Halliburton many times in the months before the *Sea Dragon* finally sailed. Sinclair was the Canadian journalist who had come to Halliburton's defense in a magazine article when others were accusing him of lying about his swim in the pool at the Taj Mahal.

Now, Sinclair was in Hong Kong to cover the war in China for the *Toronto Star*. According to Sinclair, Halliburton was "sipping innumerable cans of tomato juice and taking a few vitamin pills for his nerves." They spent many nights together during this time while Halliburton was "interlaced in troubles." Although he had spent months in Hong Kong trying to get his adventure underway and having to fight one adversity after another, according to Sinclair, Halliburton still felt he would "go forward and triumph over hardship."[151] His entire career had been built on the idea that he did things that seemed undoable. Many would tell him the thing he was about to do was too dangerous, would put his life at risk or was impossible—but each time he persevered and succeeded, and the personal and professional rewards were great. Before he returned safely home from his adventures around the world in an airplane, he was reminded many times that he was putting his life in danger each time the *Flying Carpet* took off. He must have reasoned with himself, "How is this any different?" But it was different. When he selected a pilot for the *Flying Carpet*, he was fortunate to have ended up with someone like Moye Stephens, who was able to balance out some of the more spontaneous and irresponsible aspects of Halliburton's whimsical nature that otherwise very likely would have resulted in disaster. Unfortunately, unbeknownst to Halliburton, John Welch, the man he selected as captain of the *Sea Dragon*, knew very little about building or sailing a Chinese junk, and all on board would pay dearly for that ignorance.

In his first letter, mailed from Shanghai on November 30, 1938, to those who had purchased a five-dollar membership to the "Sea Dragon Club," Halliburton introduced the members of the crew who were planning to sail with him and Welch from Hong Kong to San Francisco:

> *With the engine has come an engineer—Henry Von Fehren, born in Germany, naturalized in America.*
>
> *John "Brue" Potter graduated from Dartmouth in 1936. He has spent his summers sailing in his own 60-foot ketch up and down the Atlantic Coast. He will be our first mate. With Potter have come two of his sea-comrades, Gordon Torrey, Dartmouth '35, and Robert Chase, a senior this year at the same college.*
>
> *George Barstow, age 21, is a student of music at the Juilliard School in New York. He couldn't bring his piano along, but he did bring an enormous accordion. So he will be the* Sea Dragon's *orchestra.*
>
> *Paul Mooney, of Laguna Beach, California, is an inexperienced seaman. He happens to be a crack photographer, however. I plan to send you one of his junk pictures the moment we have a junk to*

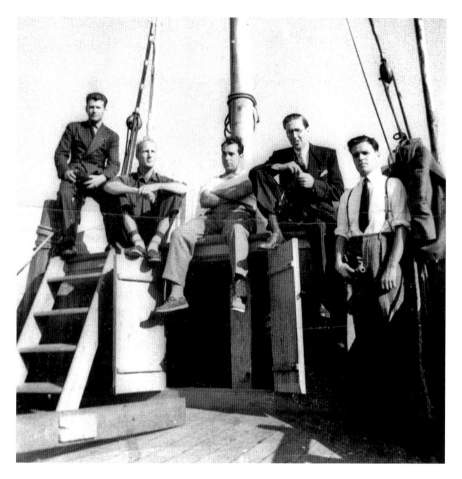

(Left to right) Paul Mooney, John Potter, George Barstow, Gordon Torrey and Robert Chase on the deck of the *Sea Dragon*. *Courtesy of the Michael E. Blankenship Collection of the Halliburton Archives, Rhodes College.*

photograph. Pictures are only a hobby with Paul, who ordinarily works as a journalist.

I hope to find a messboy in China to complete the crew. There may be a radioman too. I am still undecided.[152]

Four young, handsome college students, taking off for the "adventure of a lifetime" with a famous travel writer was great copy for the newspapers in 1938 and offered a small relief for readers from the news of 19 percent unemployment, the German occupation of Czechoslovakia and the Japanese Imperial Army overrunning Canton. Plus, Halliburton was no longer the only one working to generate press around his travels. Now he had the team at the Golden Gate International Exposition looking for ways to use him and his adventure to maximize their media coverage. When John Potter, Robert Chase, Gordon Torrey and George Barstow arrived in San Francisco, reporters were there to cover the story. The clever headline "4 Youths in a Junk" set the tone for an article that illustrated the lack of comprehension anyone really had about the real dangers of this expedition:

> *Four young men with glasses in their hands, wanderlust in their hearts and the fire of adventure in their eyes were trying to be blasé about it in San Francisco today. And each "ho hum" they emitted had more of a "heigh-ho" in it than the last. They're four students from the East en route to China where they will join Richard Halliburton, adventurer, lecturer and author and help him bring his Chinese junk back to San Francisco for the 1939 Golden Gate International Exposition…Young Potter's idea in joining the expedition is to "purge myself of wanderlust." He's been sailing since he was 8 years old, he said, and thinks its time he got the roaming fever out of himself before settling down to work at a career aimed at diplomatic service. Mr. Chase, who hails from Boston, plans to go to the Harvard business school when he returns from the Halliburton trip.*[153]

Sinclair wrote about the *Sea Dragon* in his book, *Bright Paths to Adventure*. He remembered, "There were many around that busy waterfront who said she was too heavy for her own good. Many a man told me that the junk's engine, her extra water and fuel tanks, her navigation equipment and wireless, made her too heavy for even a calm crossing of the mighty Pacific. Yet this was the season of great storms."[154]

Gordon Torrey, the "sea-comrade" of John Potter, later wrote that once he saw the *Sea Dragon* in person, he knew it was a "disaster waiting to happen."[155] Many years later, Torrey wrote to Halliburton enthusiast Michael Blankenship:

> *During the short, initial sea trial a few miles outside of Hong Kong it became apparent to me how, in the kind of seas I had seen in the Formosa Straits, while coming from Shanghai to Hong Kong in a passenger line, solid water could come right over that low spoon bow, wipe out the sky-light trunk and fill the lower deck section with enough*

> *water to enable that great heavy diesel engine to take her to the bottom. That was when I decided not to go and tried to talk Brue and Bob Chase out of going. Naturally, this led to unpleasantries and I became disassociated with the others.*[156]

On Saturday, February 4, 1939, after months of struggle, frustration, arguments and anxiety, the crew—which now included two Siamese kittens and two Chow Chow puppies—finally boarded the *Sea Dragon* and prepared to launch the ship. Chinese priests led the ceremony to "open the eyes" of the *Sea Dragon*, and the adventure had finally begun. Halliburton wrote, "After weeks of discouraging delays and false starts, our junk was ready, definitely and at last, for its great adventure. Two thousand gallons of fresh water were aboard, enough oil to fuel our auxiliary engine for ten days, and three months' supply of food for twelve men."[157]

Fourteen hours later and only one hundred miles from Hong Kong, a massive storm rolled in, and the boat was tossed around on the water like a child's toy. Most of the crew became violently seasick, John Potter was seriously injured when he was hit by the ship's boom and Paul Mooney, who didn't really want to be on the voyage in the first place, fell and broke his ankle. They had no other choice but to return to Hong Kong with a damaged ship and a disheartened and injured crew.

John Potter was rushed to the hospital in an ambulance and treated for internal injuries, which, for the media, were spun as "an appendicitis attack." Potter's injuries—or perhaps his common sense—caused him to withdraw from the voyage like Torrey had weeks before. A frustrated Paul Mooney was also taken to the hospital, where his broken ankle was put in a cast. Several others on the crew snuck away quickly, never to be heard from again. It took a month to get the *Sea Dragon* back in shape and a crew assembled and ready to tackle the voyage once again.

On March 4, 1939, the crew of the *Sea Dragon* was ready to board the junk, some for the second time. Although Paul Mooney, still in a cast, had the perfect excuse to skip the voyage, he was there that day and ready to board, crutches and all. New crewmembers had been hired to replace those who left, but the failure of the first attempt was surely on everyone's mind that day.

Gordon Sinclair was at the docks to see them off. He noticed Halliburton appeared "pretty close to a nervous breakdown" and that his face was gaunt and lined. Possibly the last person to speak to Halliburton on dry land, Sinclair shook his hand and said, "Don't get your feet wet, Dick." To which Halliburton grimly replied, "Don't take any wooden nickels."[158]

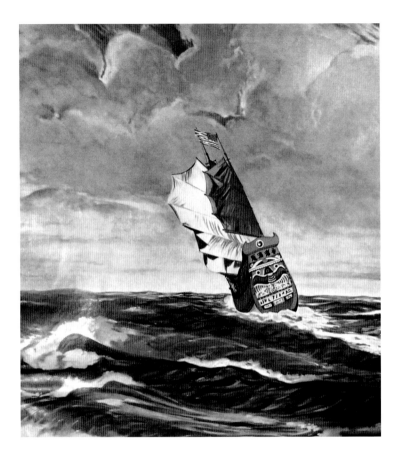

Illustration of the *Sea Dragon* used on the cover of *Richard Halliburton: His Story of His Life's Adventure*. Courtesy of the Rhodes College Archives and Special Collections, Memphis, Tennessee.

This time, the ship sailed off from the dock with no fanfare and only a handful of people, who just happened to be there, waving goodbye. Halliburton, who was used to the loud cheers of an adoring audience, received none as he departed on his last voyage. Even the local media wasn't watching this time. Other than a small note in the *South China Morning Post*, the departure of the *Sea Dragon* went unreported.[159]

For more than two weeks, the *Sea Dragon* experienced smooth sailing, and it looked like Halliburton and the crew were going to make it to San Francisco after all. It appeared that, once again, Richard Halliburton had beaten the odds. Then, on Wednesday night, March 21, a storm began. The SS *Coolidge* was close by and also experiencing the beginnings of what would become the worst typhoon many had ever experienced. The last contact with the *Sea Dragon* was received on March 23 or 24, when it was likely eight hundred miles southeast of Yokohama:

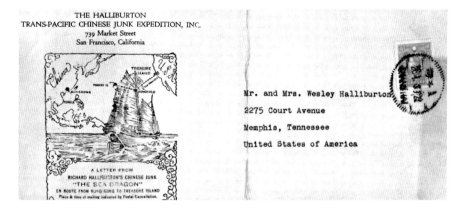

Last page of a newsletter about the *Sea Dragon* expedition, mailed to subscribers from Richard Halliburton as he prepared for the voyage. *Courtesy of the Rhodes College Archives and Special Collections, Memphis, Tennessee.*

Envelope in which Halliburton's parents received his newsletter about the *Sea Dragon* expedition. *Courtesy of the Rhodes College Archives and Special Collections, Memphis, Tennessee.*

CAPTAIN JOHN WELCH OF THE SEA DRAGON TO LINER PRESIDENT COOLIDGE SOUTHERLY GALES RAIN SQUALLS LEE RAIL UNDER WATER WET BUNKS HARDTACK BULLY BEEF HAVING WONDERFUL TIME WISH YOU WERE HERE INSTEAD OF ME

On March 25, 1939, Wesley and Nelle Halliburton were sitting in the living room of their new home in Memphis on Court Avenue when their phone rang. They looked at each other, and then Nelle Halliburton slowly answered the phone. She spoke for a moment and then returned to the living room, stood before her husband and said softly, "Well that's it. It's all over. It's the end."[160] At first, there was confusion; then there was doubt and, of course, hope. Perhaps the radio really was all that was lost and Halliburton and the others would show up at the exposition. What a story that would make! Then again, he could be up to his old tricks and counting on massive press coverage of his "disappearance." Most editors assumed it was a publicity stunt, and the articles about the missing junk were short and ended up deep on the inside of the newspapers rather than on the front pages. By the time Halliburton was declared legally dead months later, it was old news, and America was focused on the likelihood of another world war. The one newspaper that did include a fitting tribute to the late adventure writer was the *Commercial Appeal* in Memphis. Included were many of the Halliburtons' personal photos of their son and stories about his life and career.

At the end of Wesley Halliburton's life, nearly twenty-five years later, on top of a stack of old photographs and newspaper clippings in his home office sat a faded, yellow envelope that was postmarked 1939 and addressed to "Richard Halliburton, Pan-American Airways, Midway, USA." The envelope was stamped "Unclaimed," and inside was the last letter Wesley Halliburton wrote to his son. Richard Halliburton never got to read it, and the letter was returned along with many bags of other mail sent to the adventurer and intended to welcome him home. Had he arrived at the exposition and opened his father's letter, he would have read, "Since getting that wireless that you were well out, I say many times a day, 'Come on, old junk, ride the waves. Toss them about if you will, but keep coming…'"[161]

On March 3, 1939, Richard Halliburton had written one final letter before departing on the *Sea Dragon*, and it gave his grieving parents one last opportunity to hear from their son. He wrote:

> *Mother and Dad:*
> *One more—one last—goodbye letter. We sail, again, in a few hours—far more seaworthy than before. The delay has been heartbreaking, but worth it for added safety…Wilfred Crowell writes me there's a big barge anchored in the small ships' basin at the Fair and on it a big sign, "Reserved anchorage for Halliburton's* Sea Dragon.*" So we must*

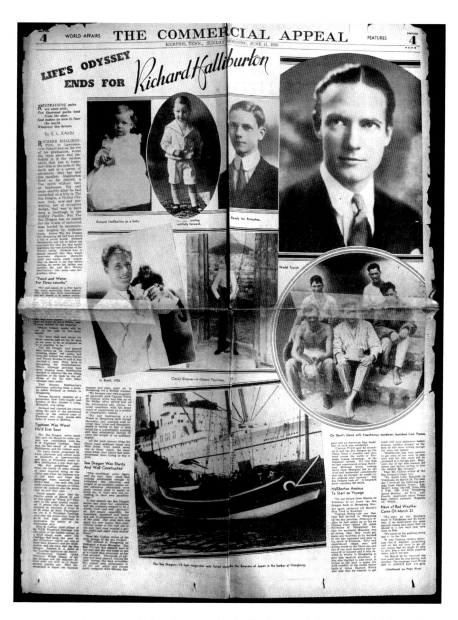

Front page of the *Commercial Appeal* on June 11, 1939. *Courtesy of the* Commercial Appeal, *Memphis, Tennessee.*

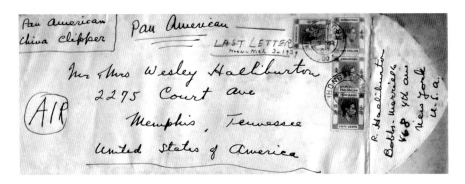

The envelope from the last letter Halliburton wrote his parents, March 3, 1939. *Courtesy of the Rhodes College Archives and Special Collections, Memphis, Tennessee.*

hurry and get there…I still think I have a swell idea, and that everything is coming out as I dreamed. But, oh, won't I be glad to get home and unload all these burdens and quarreling seamen! So goodbye again. I'll radio you every few days, so you can enjoy and follow the voyage with me. Think of it as a wonderful sport, and not as something hazardous and foolish. I embrace you and will give my sweet mother an extra hug on her birthday. You know how much I love you.
R.

Epilogue

October 9, 1939
Sad news to some of us the confirmation of Richard Halliburton's death at sea on the tiny Chinese junk…The last time Halliburton was in New York, more than two years ago, he was honor guest at a cocktail party—and among those present were O.O. McIntyre and Floyd Gibbons…Gibbons said: "The next time you go off on one of those crazy expeditions I'd like to go along, wouldn't you Odd?" McIntyre replied mildly: "Not I. We'd be fighting amongst ourselves… who'd write the trip up?"…"In a fight," chirped Halliburton, "Gibbons would win."…All three gone now.
—New York Journal American

On October 4, 1939, a jury verdict in the Chancery Court in Memphis officially declared that Richard Halliburton died on either March 23 or 24. Although his friends, family and fans around the world were heartbroken, life quickly moved on for most. Just a month earlier, Germany had invaded Poland, and soon a world at war would capture the attention of the nation.

To commemorate their son's life, Wesley and Nelle Halliburton put a small grave marker in the family plot at Forrest Hill Cemetery, next to their youngest son's grave. Under his name and year of birth and death are the words "Lost at Sea." The elder Halliburton intended to bury his son's many letters in the plot, but his niece, Juliet, convinced him it would be better to share them with the world. *Richard Halliburton: The Story of His Life's Adventures*,

EPILOGUE

a book of Halliburton's letters with additional commentary provided in large part by his father, was published in 1940. It was later discovered that before publishing the letters, Wesley Halliburton first removed, among other things, any reference to Paul Mooney that would imply that he and Halliburton had been together romantically. On the introduction page of Wesley Halliburton's copy of the book, which is now in the archives at Rhodes College, he wrote, "We characterized his other books 'our grandchildren.' But this one is indeed our beloved son, Richard. June 1940."

Wesley Halliburton officially retired from the real estate business in 1941, while his wife continued to teach psychology at Mary Hutchison's school, which she had begun in 1927. She was also one of the few practicing "psychologists" in the South, according to an article in the *Memphis Evening Appeal* written in the spring of 1928:

The mental quirks and twists of the average individual are just as clear to Mrs. Wesley Halliburton as if she possessed occult powers. By the texture of one's skin and the grip of one's hand, she senses when things are wrong. Technically speaking, Mrs. Halliburton is known as a psychologist…she has been a student of psychology for many years and recently has opened a studio in the Women's Building, where she receives clients.[162]

Mary Hutchison and Nelle Halliburton both retired from Hutchison's school in 1947, and Hutchison sold it to Dr. and Mrs. W.R. Atkinson. The Halliburtons continued to travel and spent their winters in Arizona. On the occasion of their fiftieth wedding anniversary on January 15, 1948, Halliburton wrote to the *Commercial Appeal* that he and his wife had "been going together, as man and wife, for 50 years." They had many friends, were involved in church and civic activities and continued living in their home on Court Avenue in Memphis. In November 1949, Nelle Halliburton fell at the Memphis Art Museum and broke her hip. Recovery was slow, and she was confined to her bed or a wheelchair until her death on June 19, 1955, at age eighty-six. After Richard Halliburton's death, her niece, Juliet Halliburton Davis, said that for many years, every time the phone rang, Nelle Halliburton would jump up and say, "That's Richard."[163] After Nelle Halliburton's death, Mary Hutchison wrote, "We were close friends for 63 years. She had a vivid personality and was very bright and independent in her thinking. When she once became your friend, she was loyal to the last."[164]

After his wife's death, Wesley Halliburton continued to travel and became a newspaper writer himself. He had many articles published in the same

Epilogue

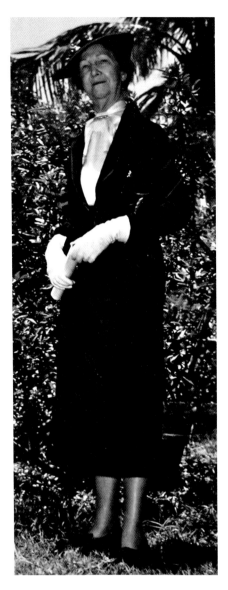

Nelle Halliburton. *Courtesy of the Rhodes College Archives and Special Collections, Memphis, Tennessee.*

Memphis newspapers that had published the articles written by his famous son. Also a frequent speaker at clubs and civic groups, Wesley Halliburton once shared his secret of longevity in one of his presentations. He said, "I attribute some of my years to the fact that I have not resisted nor forced my ways of life. Besides taking life calmly, I am sure I have added more years by my daily walks since my retirement 23 years ago, and also by denying myself the pleasure of a gourmand—I am a slight eater."[165]

At the end, Mary Hutchison and Wesley Halliburton were the last two surviving members of the little family that had begun more than sixty years earlier in Brownsville. After her retirement, Hutchison lived in a red brick house in Memphis located at 204 Dille Place. Toward the end of her life, her eyesight began failing to the point that she could no longer read, so she hired a housekeeper to read out loud to her. They had been a family of letter writers, and despite her failing eyesight, she wrote one final letter to Wesley Halliburton shortly before her death on January 30, 1962, at the age of eighty-nine. The shakiness of the nearly illegible handwriting doesn't mask the sentiment she felt toward her old friend. It read, "Hello Wesley. I feel good. Write to me soon. Love Mary." After her death, Halliburton wrote underneath her note, "My last letter from Hutchie, Jan 1962" and pasted it in the scrapbook in which he kept sentimental notes, cards and articles of significance from his family's interesting life. Hutchison was buried in the Halliburton family plot next to

Epilogue

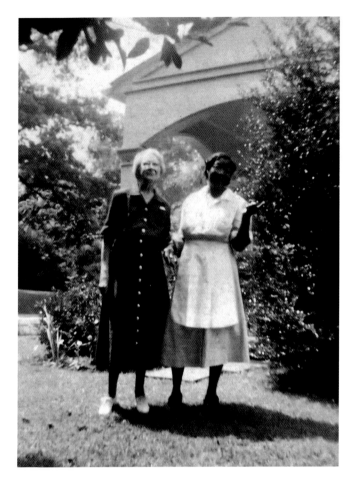

Left: Nelle Halliburton with Laura, the Halliburtons' housekeeper for more than thirty years, at the Halliburtons' home on Court Avenue. *Courtesy of the Rhodes College Archives and Special Collections, Memphis, Tennessee.*

Opposite: Painting of Mary Grimes Hutchison. The dog was added at her insistence after the painting was completed. *Photo courtesy of Hutchison School, Memphis, Tennessee.*

the graves of Nelle Halliburton and Wesley Halliburton Jr. and the headstone of Richard Halliburton. Her obituary in the *Commercial Appeal* included the tribute, "Her interests were as wide as the world, but the focal point of her love and concern was the education of her girls…life glowed within her and it radiated into every life she touched."[166] Another article stated, "In her home were the mementos of a long and fruitful life—not the least of them the many exotic objects given her by the late author-traveler Richard Halliburton. She was part of his life and he of hers."[167]

Wesley Halliburton was now alone. In 1958, James Cortese was named Sunday editor of the *Memphis Commercial Appeal*, and one of his first articles was to be about Wesley Halliburton. Fortunately, the two hit it off, and Cortese spent many nights with Halliburton and a fifth of bourbon at 2275 Court

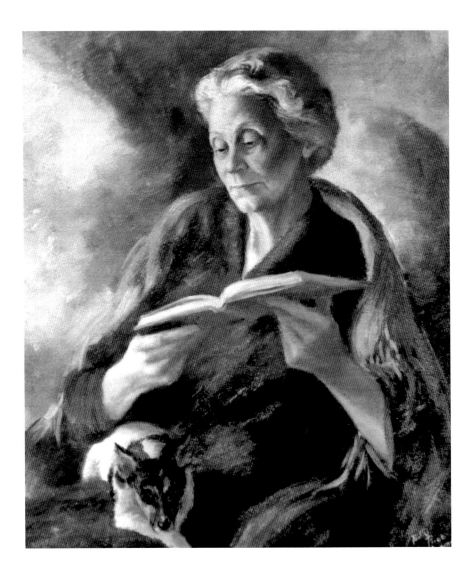

Avenue. Thanks to those many conversations and the book Cortese later wrote, *Richard Halliburton's Royal Road*, we know much more about the father and his famous son than we ever would have known otherwise. Halliburton shared much with Cortese about his decision to create a memorial tower for his son at Rhodes College. Always passionate about education, Wesley Halliburton had been instrumental in bringing Southwestern—which later become Rhodes College—to Memphis from Clarksville, Tennessee, in 1925, and he remained a strong supporter of the university through the years.

Epilogue

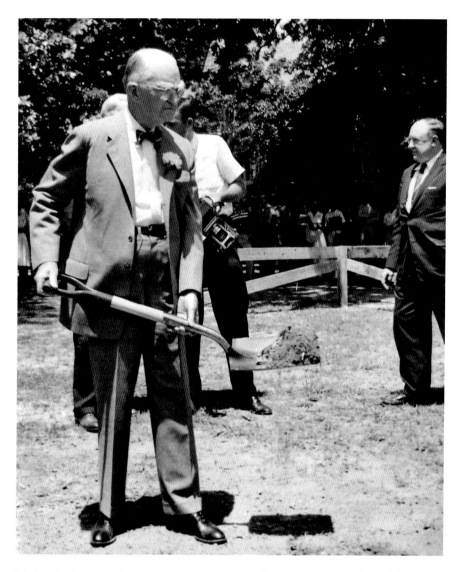

Wesley Halliburton at the groundbreaking ceremony for the Halliburton Memorial Tower at Rhodes College in Memphis. *Courtesy of the Rhodes College Archives and Special Collections, Memphis, Tennessee.*

Because of Richard Halliburton's love of Princeton, he planned to leave his entire estate there for the funding of a room for travel books, maps and charts. Wesley Halliburton told Cortese, "I got to thinking that Princeton might get $50,000 or so from Richard's estate. That's only a spit

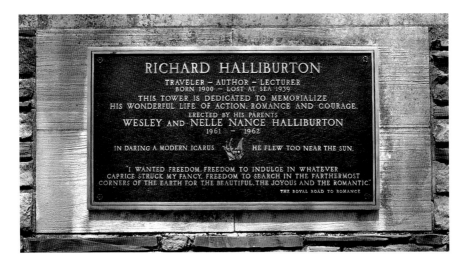

Plaque at the entrance of the Halliburton Memorial Tower at Rhodes College in Memphis. *Author's collection.*

in the ocean compared to many of the endowments that go to Princeton. I also thought that what Richard left, plus what Nelle and I left, would mean something to a small but excellent college such as Southwestern at Memphis, and she agreed."[168]

In October 1962, Wesley was there to help dedicate the Richard Halliburton Memorial Tower at Rhodes College. Cortese wrote that Halliburton looked up at the tower and remarked, "There is no ugliness here, only beauty. See how the stonework melds into the tower, like a tree roots into the ground. There is no culture in ugliness."[169]

Halliburton's final years were filled with friends, travel, writing and long walks. Of course, he did feel the painful loss of his family. One night, in the study of his home, Halliburton was reminiscing with Cortese about the past when he suddenly said softly, "I miss my Nellie." He then put his face in his hands and bent over his desk and said, "I have no Nellie now. I have no Wesley. I have no Richard."[170]

Wesley Halliburton died on November 1, 1965, at the age of ninety-five and was buried in the family plot next to his wife, youngest son and friend Mary Hutchison.

There were many others who played important, sometimes crucial roles in the creation and development of Richard Halliburton, "the daredevil adventure writer." After his death, their lives continued; some ended in

Epilogue

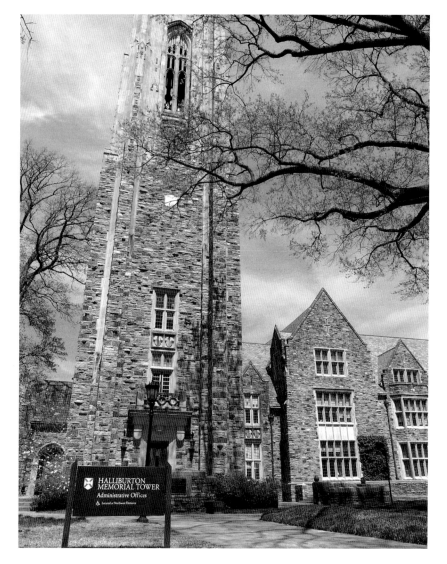

The Halliburton Memorial Tower at Rhodes College in Memphis. *Author's collection*.

tragedy, while others seemed to live happily ever after. But they all surely remembered with great fondness their time with "daring Dick."

When he wrote *The Royal Road to Romance*, Halliburton guessed what the future held for his friends and Princeton roommates, and they pretty much ended up as he had predicted. All four became leaders in their communities and lived long and happy lives. John Leh became the senior partner in his family's department store, but he also became a pioneer in aviation. In 1928, he and his wife were the second married couple in the United States to both have a pilot's license. He died in 1985. James Seiberling followed up Princeton with the University of Michigan Law School and eventually succeeded his father as president of the Seiberling Rubber Company. He died in 1982. Like his father and grandfather before him, Dr. Larry Keyes became a successful physician in Kansas City, where he remained until his death in 1990. Irvine Hockaday became a stockbroker and served as a director and trustee for many educational, civic and financial organizations until his death in 1993.

David Laurance Chambers, who worked so closely with Halliburton on all his books, continued his role leading Bobbs-Merrill until 1953. He had been with the publisher for fifty years and had written several books himself, including *The Metre of Macbeth* and *Indiana: A Hoosier History*. Thomas D. Clark, another of the writers with whom Chambers worked, wrote about a visit he paid to Chambers shortly before the publishing executive's death. It's tempting to think that, had Halliburton lived, this could have been his encounter with Chambers.

> *Upon occasion when I was in Indianapolis, I stopped by the Bobbs-Merrill office to visit him. He was in retirement but still came to the office. The last time I saw him he asked me to come around the desk and sit by his side. We had a long conversation about authors and books, and when I got up to go he put his arm around my neck and gave me a fatherly pat.*[171]

Chambers died at his home on his eighty-fourth birthday in 1962.

If anyone could be credited with "discovering" Richard Halliburton first, it would be William B. Feakins, who gave him a shot as a lecturer. By 1946, Feakins had been in the talent management business for forty years. He was credited with creating what was referred to at the time as the "Ice Age of the American Lecture Field" by managing the speaking careers of polar region explorers like Commodore Oliver Hazard and Sir Wilfred T. Grenfell. In the spring of 1946, he was working on a speaking tour for Randolph Churchill, the son of the British prime minister, when Feakins unexpectedly died at his home at the age of seventy-four.

Moye Stephens, Pancho Barnes and Elly Beinhorn all lived to see old age. After his *Flying Carpet* adventure, Stephens became an inaugural member of the Los Angeles County Sheriff's Aero Squadron and a founder of the

Aviation Country Club of California. In 1989, after a lifetime of flying and working in many different areas of aviation, he was elected to the OX-5 Aviation Pioneers Hall of Fame, where he joined Charles Lindbergh, Howard Hughes, Jimmy Doolittle and fifty other eminent individuals in the aerospace field. Stephens died in 1995.

Pancho Barnes continued her outrageous lifestyle, and after losing most of her money in the Depression, she used what little she had left to purchase 180 acres of land in the Mojave Desert near March Army Air Base. She built a dude ranch and bar of some notoriety called the Happy Bottom Riding Club. Eventually, the Reverend Barnes granted her the divorce she wanted, and she went on to marry three more times. Barnes died in March 1975 at the age of seventy-four, isolated and alone.

For her flights from Germany to Africa in 1931 and to Australia in 1932, Elly Beinhorn was awarded the Hindenburg Cup from the German aeronautical industry, which included a large cash prize. She continued to fly and became a frequent lecturer around Germany and Czechoslovakia. In 1936, she married handsome racecar driver Bernd Rosemeyer, and together they became a celebrity couple popular with the Nazi party. Their happiness together was short-lived, as Rosemeyer was killed while attempting to break a speed record just ten weeks after the birth of their son. Beinhorn remarried and continued flying until the age of seventy-two in 1979. She died in November 2007 at the age of one hundred.

The deathbed confession Halliburton heard from Ermakov in Russia turned out to be neither a real confession nor a real deathbed. The entire thing was a "deliberately stage-managed act of misinformation…set up by the secret police."[172] Ermakov did die, but in 1952, seventeen years after giving Halliburton a story that, at best, contained significant untruths.

Although Richard Halliburton never got the opportunity to finish his book on Rupert Brooke, Canadian poet and novelist Arthur Stringer heard about the research he had compiled, contacted Wesley Halliburton and was given permission to use the materials to write *Red Wine of Youth: A Life of Rupert Brooke*. The book Halliburton hoped to write was finally published by Bobbs-Merrill in 1948. As was written in the opening chapter, "The adventurer who once braved the Sahara and once climbed Mount Olympus met a death

Opposite, top: The Hangover House in 2011. *Courtesy Jeff Boyd.*

Opposite, bottom: Richard Halliburton historical marker in Brownsville, Tennessee. *Author's collection.*

Epilogue

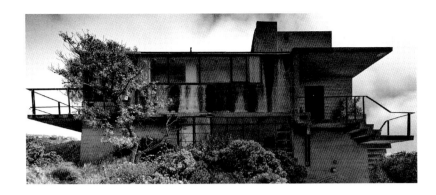

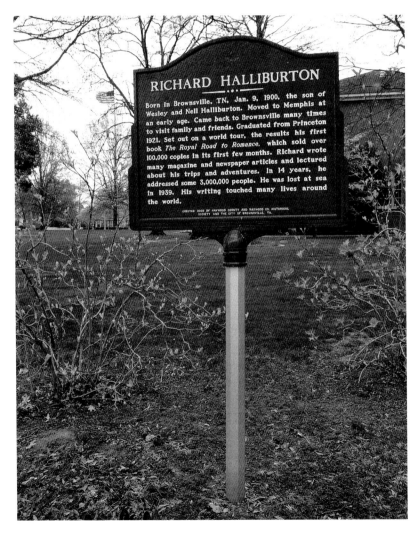

at sea as untimely and tragic as the earlier death he had proposed to write about. And the accumulated material was passed on to other hands."[173]

After completing Hangover House, William Alexander designed a few other unique homes, including a house in Encino for scriptwriter David Greggory and a house he built for himself in the Hollywood Hills called the "House in Space." In 1952, weary of dealing with the construction business, Alexander opened The Mart on Santa Monica Boulevard. It was one of the first art and antique boutiques in Los Angeles. He became so well known for his enthusiastic support of the arts in Los Angeles that when he died on June 2, 1997, few even knew of his connection to Richard Halliburton and Hangover House.

Like the friends and family in Halliburton's life, Hangover House also began to age. For the Halliburtons, Hangover House had been a part of their son's life they would have preferred never happened. For a few years, various tenants rented the house, and then in 1942, they sold it at auction to Wallace and Zolita Scott for just $9,000. After her husband's death, Zolita continued to live in the house until she died in November 2010. It then sat empty for a period of time and became extremely run down and was quickly deteriorating. It finally sold for a little over $3 million in December 2011, and the new owners began the process of restoring Halliburton's former home.

The great adventure writer and his family, friends and most of his original fans are now gone and will continue to fade further into history with each passing decade. But perhaps Wesley Halliburton was wrong when he compared his son to a meteor that blazed across the heavens and then was gone. Richard Halliburton may have perished during that storm in the Pacific Ocean, but the written words he left behind can continue to inspire future generations to cast aside the "even tenor" and embrace a life of travel and adventure.

Notes

Preface

1. Schwartz, "Richard Halliburton: The Ultimate Tourist."
2. Townsend, "Richard Halliburton: The Forgotten Myth."
3. Cortese, *Halliburton's Royal Road*, 8.

Chapter 1

4. John Wesley Halliburton to Juliet Halliburton, March 6, 1861, Folder 2, John Wesley Halliburton Papers, 1861.
5. John Wesley Halliburton to Juliet Halliburton, April 22, 1861, Folder 2, John Wesley Halliburton Papers, 1861.
6. Cortese, *Halliburton's Royal Road*, 14.
7. Halliburton, "Paul Flowers' Greenhouse."
8. Rutherford, *Genealogical History*, 148.
9. *Commercial Appeal*, "In the Social Realm," January 24, 1898.
10. Halliburton, *New Worlds to Conquer*, 331.
11. Talley, "Rich in City's Traditions, Nineteenth Century Club is Cultural Pattern."
12. Wesley Halliburton, speech given to friends, December 27, 1935.

Chapter 2

13. Frey and Frey, *Reflections on Learning and Life*, 2.
14. Ibid., 8.
15. Ibid., 3.
16. Halliburton, *Story of His Life's Adventure*, 2.

Chapter 3

17. The Battle Creek Sanitarium did a great deal of advertising and promotion throughout its history, and ads can be found in newspapers and magazines, especially around the turn of the century.
18. *Annual Report of the Battle Creek Sanitarium and Hospital*, 13.
19. Halliburton, *Letters*, 7.
20. From Wesley Halliburton's death certificate.
21. Cortese, *Halliburton's Royal Road*, 50.
22. Taylor, *Shooting Star*, 239.
23. Halliburton, *Letters*, 80.

Chapter 4

24. Ibid., 22.
25. Ibid.
26. Ibid., 20.
27. Deffaa, "On the Trail of Richard Halliburton."
28. Halliburton, *Letters*, 51.
29. Ibid., 31.

Chapter 5

30. Sargent, *Handbook of American Private Schools*, 92.
31. The Lawrenceville School. "Buildings and Grounds Collection." http://stephanarchives.org/doing-research/collections/finding-aids/buildings-and-grounds-collection-finding-aid (accessed May 26, 2014).
32. Halliburton, *Letters*, 74.
33. Karabel, *The Chosen*, 60.

34. Kemeny, "President Francis Landley Patton, Princeton University, and Faculty Ferment."
35. Bryer et al., *F. Scott Fitzgerald*, 49.
36. Halliburton, *Letters*, 15.
37. Ibid.

Chapter 6

38. Halliburton, *Royal Road to Romance*, 2.
39. Jefferson, *Notes on the State of Virginia*, 17.
40. Halliburton, *Letters*, 57.
41. *Michigan Alumnus*, "The Royal Road to Romance."
42. Halliburton, *Letters*, 62.
43. Ibid., 69.
44. Ibid., 67.
45. Flowers, "Memphis Odyssey Revived," *Commercial Appeal*, December 7, 1952.
46. Halliburton, *Letters*, 80.
47. Taylor, *Shooting Star*, 237.

Chapter 7

48. Simon J. McPherson Papers, Lawrenceville School Stephan Archives, http://stephanarchives.org/doing-research/collections/finding-aids/simon-j-mcpherson-papers-finding-aid.
49. Cortese, *Halliburton's Royal Road*, 89.
50. Halliburton, *Letters*, 208.

Chapter 8

51. Baughman, *American Decades*.
52. Halliburton, *Letters*, 209.
53. Ibid., 210.
54. *The Lyceum*, "Whereahiko Rawei," April 1923, 49.
55. Halliburton, *Letters*, 213.
56. Halliburton, article in the *Commercial Appeal*, July 16, 1922, 1.

57. Halliburton, *Letters*, 214
58. *The Survey* (New York: Survey Associates Inc., 1919).

Chapter 9

59. Halliburton, *Letters*, 225
60. Ibid., 221.
61. Ibid., 222.
62. Ibid.
63. Ibid., 230.
64. Ibid., 232.
65. Ibid., 220
66. Ibid., 234.
67. Ibid., 235.
68. Fisher, *How to Live*, 85.
69. Ibid., ix.
70. Ibid., 1.

Chapter 10

71. Root, *Magnificent Myth*, 105.
72. Bodenhamer and Barrows, *Encyclopedia of Indianapolis*, 992.
73. Cortese, *Halliburton's Royal Road*, 103
74. Ibid.
75. Halliburton, *Letters*, 241
76. Clark, "David Laurence Chambers as I Knew Him," 100.
77. Root, *Magnificent Myth*, 106.

Chapter 11

78. Taylor, *Shooting Star*, 76.
79. Halliburton, *Glorious Adventure*, 115.

Chapter 12

80. Ibid., *Royal Road to Romance*, 173.
81. Corey Ford, "The Adventure Racket."
82. Halliburton, *Letters*, 259–60.
83. Duke, "Richard Halliburton."
84. *New Bedford Massachusetts Standard*, "Talk Sparkles with More Zest than Could Be Put into a Book."
85. *Rocky Mountain News*, "Feminine Hearts Flutter over Romantic Vagabond."
86. Crowther, "Halliburton Is Well Received."
87. Halliburton, *Letters*, 279.
88. Ibid., 262.
89. Vanity Fair, "We Nominate for Oblivion," June 1930, 49.
90. Halliburton, *Letters*, 271.

Chapter 13

91. Ibid., 284.
92. Halliburton, *New Worlds to Conquer*, 114
93. Ibid., *Letters*, 291.
94. *Worchester (MA) Telegram*, "On Tour with Halliburton."
95. Ibid.
96. Ibid.

Chapter 14

97. Riddell, "New Ladies' Clubs to Conquer."
98. Halliburton, *Letters*, 271.
99. Max, "Richard Halliburton and Thomas Wolfe."
100. Marion Leland, "Tea-Cup Confessions," *Brooklyn Eagle*, May 9, 1928.
101. Dayton, "Richard Halliburton, 'Prince of Lovers,' Talks about Women and Love."
102. Sieve, "The Fourth Tea Table Debate."
103. Ibid.

Chapter 15

104. Sullivan, *Our Times*, vol. II, 556–57.
105. Pisano, *Airplane in American Culture*, 21.
106. Halliburton, *Letters*, 307.
107. Schultz, *Flying Carpets, Flying Wings*, 123–24.
108. Max, *Horizon Chasers*, 70.
109. Schultz, *Flying Carpets, Flying Wings*, 141.
110. Cortese, *Halliburton's Royal Road*, 124.
111. Schultz, *Flying Carpets, Flying Wings*, 238.
112. *Los Angeles California News*, "The Flying Carpet," February 13, 1932.
113. Taylor, *Shooting Star*, 139.
114. Ibid., 136.
115. Schultz, *Flying Carpets, Flying Wings*, 205–06.
116. Ibid., 221.
117. Beinhorn, *Flying Girl*, 4–5.
118. Ibid.
119. Halliburton, *Letters*, 338.
120. Root, *Magnificent Myth*, 210.

Chapter 16

121. Halliburton, *Letters*, 341.
122. Pitts, *Columbia Pictures*, 3.
123. Ibid.
124. Halliburton, *Letters*, 342.
125. Max, *Horizon*, 31.
126. Halliburton, *Letters*, 306.
127. Mark Dowling, "World-Explorer Discovers America," date and publication unknown.

Chapter 17

128. Halliburton, *Seven League Boots*, 15.
129. Ibid., *Letters*, 358.
130. Ibid.

131. Halliburton, *Seven League Boots*, 144.
132. Ibid., *Letters*, 359–60.
133. Ibid., *Seven League Boots*, 417.

Chapter 18

134. Ibid., *Letters*, 383.
135. Max, *Horizon*, 171.
136. Denzer, "The Halliburton House and Its Architect," 328.
137. Halliburton, *Letters*, 389.
138. Ibid., 386.
139. Ibid., 390.
140. Denzer, "The Halliburton House and Its Architect," 328.
141. Halliburton, *Letters*, 391.
142. Denzer, "The Halliburton House and Its Architect," 328.

Chapter 19

143. *Indianapolis Star*, "President of Bobbs-Merrill Discloses Halliburton Believed Safe on Pacific," April 20, 1939.
144. Barron, Bernstein and Susan, *Reading California*, 76.
145. Art Linkletter with Dean Jennings, *Confessions of a Happy Man* (New York: Pocket Books Inc., 1960), 109.
146. Hilmes, *Radio Voices*, 183.
147. Phelen, "Halliburton's Banana Peel," 80.
148. Ibid., 105.
149. Halliburton, *Letters*, 402.
150. Richard Halliburton, "Sea Dragon," *Buffalo News*, April 22, 1939.
151. Sinclair, *Bright Paths to Adventure*, 93.
152. Richard Halliburton, letter from the archives at Rhodes College.
153. *San Francisco News*, "4 Youths in a Junk," October 20, 1938.
154. Sinclair, *Bright Paths to Adventure*, 97.
155. Cortese, *Halliburton's Royal Road*, 177.
156. Ibid., 178.
157. Halliburton, *Letters*, 425.
158. Sinclair, *Bright Paths to Adventure*, 98.

159. *South China Morning Post*, "Richard Halliburton: The Hero Time Forgot."
160. Root, *Magnificent Myth*, 268.
161. Whited, "A Restless Rebel on the Royal Road," 12.

Epilogue

162. York, "Would Cure Human Ills by Practical Psychology."
163. Taylor, *Shooting Star*, 239.
164. *Memphis Commercial Appeal*, "Mrs. Halliburton, Noted Memphian, Dies at Her Home."
165. Notes written by nephew Gus Halliburton on April 28, 1964, and in Halliburton archives.
166. Frey and Frey, *Reflections on Learning and Life*, 52.
167. *Memphis Press-Scimitar*, "Miss Mary Hutchison," January 31, 1962.
168. Cortese, *Halliburton's Royal Road*, 169.
169. Ibid., 170.
170. Ibid., 172.
171. Clark, "David Laurence Chambers as I Knew Him," 106.
172. Rappaport, *Last Days of the Romanovs*, 215.
173. Stringer, *Red Wine of Youth*, 23.

Bibliography

BOOKS

Adams, Mark. *Mr. America*. New York: Harper Collins, 2009.

Alt, John H. *Don't Die in Bed: The Brief Intense Life of Richard Halliburton*. Atlanta, GA: Quincunx Press, 2013.

Axtell, James. *The Making of Princeton University*. Princeton, NJ: Princeton University Press, 2006.

Barron, Stephanie, Sheri Bernstein and Ilene Susan. *Reading California: Art, Image, and Identity, 1900–2000*. Oakland: University of California Press, 2000.

Baughman, Judith S. *Decades, 1920–1929*. New York: Gale Research Inc., 1995.

Beinhorn, Elly. *Flying Girl*. London: Geoffrey Bles, 1935.

Bodenhamer, David J., and Robert G. Barrows. *The Encyclopedia of Indianapolis*. Bloomington: Indiana University Press, 1994.

Boyer, Paul S., and Melvyn Dubofsky. *The Oxford Companion to United States History*. New York: Oxford University Press, 2001.

Bibliography

Brownsville-Haywood County Bicentennial Book Committee. *Heart of the Tennessee Delta: A Historical Guidebook to Haywood County*. N.p.: Dixie Printing Company, 1996.

Bryer, Jackson R., Alan Margolies and Ruth Prigozy. *F. Scott Fitzgerald: New Perspectives*. Athens: University of Georgia Press, 2000.

Cortese, James. *Richard Halliburton's Royal Road*. Memphis, TN: White Rose Press, 1989.

Drowne, Kathleen, and Patrick Huber. *American Popular Culture through History*. Westport, CT: Greenville Press, 2004.

Edge, Laura B. *From Jazz Babies to Generation Next: The History of the American Teenager*. Minneapolis, MN: Twenty-First Century Books, 2011.

Endres, Kathleen L., and Therese L. Lueck. *Women's Periodicals in the United States: Consumer Magazines*. Westport, CT: Greenwood Publishing Group, 1995.

Fisher, Irving. *Rules for Healthful Living Based on Science*. New York and London: Funk & Wagnalls Company, 1916.

Frey, Sarah A., and Leonard W. Frey. *Reflections on Learning and Life and Hutchison School*. Memphis, TN: Hutchison School, 2003.

Halliburton, Richard. *Book of Marvels: The Occident*. Indianapolis and New York: Bobbs-Merrill, 1937.

———. *The Flying Carpet*. Indianapolis and New York: Bobbs-Merrill, 1932.

———. *The Glorious Adventure*. Indianapolis and New York: Bobbs-Merrill, 1927.

———. *New Worlds to Conquer*. Indianapolis and New York: Bobbs-Merrill, 1929.

———. *Richard Halliburton: His Story of His Life's Adventure*. New York: Bobbs-Merrill, 1940.

———. *The Royal Road to Romance*. Indianapolis and New York: Bobbs-Merrill, 1925.

———. *Second Book of Marvels: The Orient*. Indianapolis and New York: Bobbs-Merrill, 1938.

———. *Seven League Boots*. Indianapolis and New York: Bobbs-Merrill, 1935.

Hamilton, John Maxwell. *Journalism's Roving Eye*. Baton Rouge: Louisiana State University Press, 2009.

Hilmes, Michele. *Radio Voices: American Broadcasting, 1922–1952*. Minneapolis: University of Minnesota Press, 1997.

Jefferson, Thomas. *Notes on the State of Virginia*. Richmond, VA: J.W. Randolph, 1853.

Johnson, Owen. *The Varmint*. New York: A.L. Burt Co., 1910.

Karabel, Jerome. *The Chosen: The Hidden History of Admission and Exclusion at Harvard, Yale, and Princeton*. New York: Houghton Mifflin, 2005.

Kessler, Lauren. *The Happy Bottom Riding Club: The Life and Times of Pancho Barnes*. New York: Random House, 2000.

Linkletter, Art. *Confessions of a Happy Man*. New York: Random House, 1960.

Macleod, David I. *Building Character in the American Boy*. Madison: Wisconsin Press, 1983.

Max, Gerry. *The Lives and Adventures of Richard Halliburton and Paul Mooney*. Jefferson, NC: McFarland & Company Inc., 2007.

Middleton, Kathleen M. *Lawrence Township*. Charleston, SC: Arcadia Publishing, 1994.

O'Bar, Jack. *The Origins and History of the Bobbs-Merrill Company*. Urbana: University of Illinois Press, 1985.

O'Neal, Michael J. *Decades of American History: America in the 1920s*. New York: Stonesong Press, 2006.

Pisano, Dominick. *The Airplane in American Culture*. Ann Arbor: University of Michigan Press, 2003.

Pitts, Michael R. *Columbia Pictures Horror, Science Fiction and Fantasy Films, 1928–1982*. Jefferson, NC: McFarland, 2010.

Rappaport, Helen. *The Last Days of the Romanovs: Tragedy at Ekaterinburg*. New York: St. Martin's Press, 2008.

Root, Jonathan. *Halliburton: The Magnificent Myth*. New York: Coward-McCann Inc., 1965.

Rubin, Joan Shelly, and Scott E. Casper. *The Oxford Encyclopedia*. New York: Oxford University Press, 2013.

Rutherford, William Kenneth, and Anna Clay Zimmerman Rutherford. *Genealogical History of the Halliburton Family*. Madison, WI: Brown-White-Lowell Press, 1959.

Sargent, Potter E. *The Handbook of American Private Schools*. Boston: P. Sargent, 1916.

Schultz, Barbara H. *Flying Carpets, Flying Wings: The Biography of Moye W. Stephens*. Lancaster, CA: Little Buttes Publishing Co., 2010.

Sinclair, Gordon. *Bright Paths to Adventure*. Toronto: McClelland and Stewart Publishers, 1945.

Streissguth, Thomas. *The Roaring Twenties*. New York: Infobase Publishing, 2007.

Stringer, Arthur. *Red Wine of Youth: A Life of Rupert Brooke*. Indianapolis, IN: Bobbs-Merrill Co., 1949.

Studlar, Gaylyn. *The Mad Masquerade: Stardom and Masculinity in the Jazz Age*. New York: Columbia University Press, 1996.

Sullivan, Mark. *Our Times: The United States, 1900–1925.* New York: Charles Scribner's Sons, 1928.

Taylor, William R. *A Shooting Star Meets the Well of Death.* Abbeville, SC: Moonshine Cove Publishing, 2013.

Periodicals and Other Sources

Booth, Clare. "We Nominate for Oblivion." *Vanity Fair,* June 1930, 49.

Clark, Thomas D. "David Laurence Chambers as I Knew Him." *Indiana Bookman,* no. 8 (1967): 100–06.

Commercial Appeal. "In the Social Realm." January 27, 1898.

———. "Mrs. Halliburton, Noted Memphian, Dies at Her Home." June 20, 1955, 11.

———. "Wesley Halliburton Dies: Writer, Traveler, Engineer." November 2, 1965, A1.

Crowther, Rodney. "Halliburton Is Well Received." *Asheville Citizen,* April 20, 1928, 1.

Dayton, Dorothy. "Richard Halliburton, 'Prince of Lovers,' Talks about Women and Love." *Illustrated Love,* March 1930, 41.

Deffaa, Chip. "On the Trail of Richard Halliburton." *Princeton Alumni Weekly,* May 13, 1975, 8.

Denzer, Anthony. "The Halliburton House and Its Architect, William Alexander." *Southern California Quarterly* 91, no. 3 (Fall 2009): 319–41.

Duke, Mabel. "Richard Halliburton." *Dallas Texas Dispatch,* January 18, 1928.

Evening Independent. "Indiana Writers Developed by New Editor of Century." October 12, 1925, A2.

Flowers, Paul. "Memphis Odyssey Revived." *Commercial Appeal*, December 7, 1952.

Ford, Corey. "The Adventure Racket." *Vanity Fair*, July 1929, 35.

Franklin, Mortimer. "Who Said No More Thrills?" *Screenland*, April 1933, 61.

Ginsburg, Ted. "Richard Halliburton's Adventures, Revised." *English Journal* 27, no. 6 (June 1938): 507–09.

Hahn, Rebekka. "Mass Media in the 1920s." Seminar paper, Johannes Gutenberg University Mainz, 2008.

Halliburton, Richard. "Christmas Dinner Around the World." *Cosmopolitan*, January 1936, 57.

Halliburton, Wesley. "Paul Flowers' Greenhouse." *Commercial Appeal*, January 20, 1953.

Herald Statesman. "W.B. Feakins, Lecture Bureau Manager, Dies." March 26, 1946, 2.

Hirshbein, Laura Davidow. "Masculinity, Work, and the Fountain of Youth: Irving Fisher and the Life Extension Institute." *Canadian Bulletin of Medical History* 16 (1999): 89–124.

Kemeny, Paul C. "President Francis Landley Patton, Princeton University, and Faculty Ferment." *American Presbyterians* (1991): 111–21.

Leland, Marion. "Tea-Cup Confessions." *Brooklyn Eagle*, May 9, 1928.

Look. "Inside the House That Richard Halliburton Built." December 19, 1939.

The Lyceum. "Whereahiko Rawei." April 1923, 49.

Max, Gerry. "Richard Halliburton and Thomas Wolfe: When Youth Kept Open House." *North Carolina Literary Review* 5 (1996): 92.

Michigan Alumnus. "The Royal Road to Romance." December 4, 1926, 208.

Morris, Charles E., III. "Richard Halliburton's Bearded Tales." *Quarterly Journal of Speech* 95 (May 2009): 123–47.

New Bedford Massachusetts Standard. "Talk Sparkles with More Zest than Could Be Put into a Book." March 31, 1928.

Newsweek. "Halliburton Rides Again." November 20, 1961, 31.

———. "Richard Halliburton." October 16, 1939, 31.

Princeton Alumni Weekly. "Letters Home." October 21, 1940, 7.

———. "The Royal Road to Romance." December 13, 1929, 335.

Quinn, Olive. "Richard Halliburton, Prominent Author, Interviewed by *Ridge Echo* Reporter." *Ridge Echo*, May 5, 1933, 1.

Rabbitt, Jennifer. "A Home for the Soul." *Orange County*, September 1989, 22.

Riddell, John [Corey Ford]. "New Ladies' Clubs to Conquer." *Vanity Fair*, September 1928, 73.

Rocky Mountain News. "Feminine Hearts Flutter over Romantic Vagabond." March 16 1929.

San Francisco News. "4 Youths in a Junk." October 20, 1938.

Schwartz, David M. "On the Royal Road to Adventures with 'Daring Dick.'" *Smithsonian*, March 1989, 159.

———. "Richard Halliburton: The Ultimate Tourist." *Smithsonian* 19, no. 12 (March 1989): 159–78.

Sieve, Myriam. "The Fourth Tea Table Debate." *Home Magazine*, 1930.

Sontag, Susan. "Homage to Halliburton." *Oxford American*, March April 2001, 120.

South China Morning Post. "Richard Halliburton: The Hero Time Forgot." March 23, 2014, 1.

Time. "Last Adventure." June 19, 1939, 59.

Townsend, Guy. "Richard Halliburton: The Forgotten Myth." *City of Memphis*, August 1977, 33.

Vogue. "Halliburton's Banana Peel." February 1, 1969, 64.

Walton, Lloyd B. "Volumes of Memories." *S Magazine*, September 7, 1975, 10.

Weller, George. "The Passing of the Last Playboy." *Esquire*, April 1940, 58.

Whited, Charles. "A Restless Rebel on the Royal Road." *The Nashville Tennesseean*, October 23, 1960, 12.

Worcester (MA) Telegram. "On Tour with Halliburton." January 26, 1930.

York, Mary. "Would Cure Human Ills by Practical Psychology." *Memphis Evening Appeal*, March 1, 1928.

Websites

Princeton University. "A Brief History of the Development and Evolution of the Eating Club System at Princeton University." http://www.princeton.edu/ectf/docs/TaskForceHistory.pdf.

———. "The Presidents of Princeton University." http://www.princeton.edu/pub/presidents/.

Who's Who in TN. "Thomas, Spencer F." http://tngenweb.org/whos-who/thomas-spencer-f/.

Bibliography

Films

The Happy Years. DVD. Directed by William A. Wellman. Los Angeles, CA: Metro-Goldwyn-Mayer Studios, 1950.

The Legend of Pancho Barnes and the Happy Bottom Riding Club. DVD. Written and produced by Nick T. Spark; directed by Amanda Pope. Los Angeles, CA: Nick Spark Productions, 2009.

Le Passage du Grand-Saint-Bernard à dos d'éléphant. St-Maurice: Archivalp Patrimoine Audiovisuel des Alpes, 2011. http://vimeo.com/16056840.

Collections

Booth Tarkington to George Ade, May 8, 1924. Box 10, Folder 5, George Ade Papers, 1878–2007. Virginia Kelly Karnes Archives and Special Collections Research Center, Purdue University Libraries, West Lafayette, IN.

Letters from John Wesley Halliburton, 1861. Collection #4414-z, John Wesley Halliburton Papers, 1861. Southern Historical Collection, University of North Carolina, Chapel Hill.

Index

A

Africa Speaks! 122, 123
Alexander, William 134, 135, 136, 137, 138, 139, 141, 170
Athens Female College 19

B

Barnes, Florence "Pancho" 109, 110, 111, 167, 168
Barstow, George 150, 151, 152
Battle Creek Sanitarium 27, 28, 29, 31, 39, 69
Beinhorn, Elly 116, 117, 118, 119, 167, 168
Bobbs-Merrill 70, 71, 72, 73, 87, 96, 97, 106, 107, 127, 128, 167, 168
Bond, Carrie Jacobs 85
Book of Marvels 144, 145, 146
Boy Scouts 62, 63
Brooke, Rupert 76, 78, 87, 91, 98, 105, 114, 168
Brown, Rosie 123
Brownsville, Tennessee 15, 19, 20, 21, 22, 23, 25, 34, 35, 161, 169
Byron, Lord 75

C

Chambers, David Laurance 70, 71, 72, 73, 74, 76, 91, 106, 127, 135, 142, 144, 167
Chaplin, Charlie 10, 14, 37, 38, 58, 125, 134
Chase and Sanborn's Coffee 88
Chase, Robert 147, 150, 151, 152, 153
Chichen Itza 10, 91
Commercial Appeal 15, 34, 62, 160
Cortese, James 32, 111, 162, 163, 164, 165
Coward, Tim 70, 72, 73
Curtis, Cyrus 90

D

Dalrymple, Elysabethe 129, 131, 132
Davis, Juliet Halliburton 33, 52, 159
Devil's Island 10, 91, 95

INDEX

Dewitt, Arkansas 17, 18
Drayton, Grace 85, 86

E

Earhart, Amelia 10, 14
Ermakov, Peter Zacharovitch 130, 168

F

Fairbanks, Douglass 58, 67, 134
Feakins, Albert 61, 62, 63
Feakins Lecture Bureau 63
Feakins, William B. 61, 63, 64, 67, 69, 72, 76, 167
Fisher, Irving 49, 68, 69
Fitzgerald, F. Scott 10, 14, 42, 43, 44, 85
Flying Carpet 10, 104, 110, 111, 115, 118, 121, 123, 124, 127, 150, 167
Ford, Corey 82, 83, 101
Forrest Hill Cemetery 159, 161, 165
Franck, Harry 46, 49
Futter, Walter and Fred 122, 123, 126

G

Gaul, George 76, 77
Gibraltar 10, 55
Glorious Adventure, The 87, 105
Golden Gate International Exposition 14, 94, 143, 144, 152
Guinness World Record 94

H

Halliburton, Colonel William H. 18, 19
Halliburton, Erle 111, 147
Halliburton, John Wesley 15, 16, 17
Halliburton, Juliet 15, 18
Halliburton, Nelle 19, 20, 21, 22, 24, 25, 32, 34, 35, 76, 77, 87, 156, 159, 160, 161, 162, 165
Halliburton, Wesley 14, 17, 19, 21, 25, 28, 35, 46, 48, 49, 52, 55, 56, 67, 87, 103, 106, 111, 123, 142, 156, 160, 161, 162, 163, 164, 165, 168, 170
Halliburton, Wesley, Jr. 21, 22, 23, 31, 32, 33
Halliburton, Zola 147
Hangover House 133, 134, 135, 137, 139, 140, 141, 146, 147, 170
Harpers Ferry 46, 47, 49, 50
Harriman, Averell 54
Haywood County 15, 16, 17, 19, 20, 45
Hellespont 10, 75, 87, 102, 144
Hockaday, Irvine O. "Mike" 40, 47, 52, 54, 55, 167
Hong Kong 9, 14, 147, 149, 150, 152, 153
Howland, Hewitt Hanson 73, 74
Hutchison, Mary 23, 24, 26, 27, 68, 77, 78, 106, 128, 160, 161, 162, 165
Hutchison School 24, 25, 160

I

India Speaks! 123, 124, 126, 127
Ipswich 54, 55

K

Kahanamoku, Duke 120, 121
Kellogg, John Harvey 28, 69
Keyes, Edward L. "Larry" 40, 47, 167

L

Ladies Home Journal 59, 89, 90, 91, 95, 97, 98, 106, 112
Laguna Beach 133, 134, 137, 139, 146, 150
Lawrenceville School 29, 31, 32, 39, 40, 41, 42, 46, 50, 53, 54, 76, 78
Leh, John Henry "Heinie" 40, 46, 167
Ley, Harold 68
Life Extension Institute 68, 69
Lindbergh, Charles 14, 105, 168
Linkletter, Art 144
Luce, Booth Clare 88, 90

Index

M

Matterhorn 10, 55, 122
McPherson, Lucy Belle Harmon 54
McPherson, Reverend Simon John 53, 54
Memphis Press-Scimitar 57, 64, 142
Memphis University School 23
Merrill, Samuel 71
Mooney, Charles Joseph Patrick 62
Mooney, Paul 62, 111, 123, 124, 135, 136, 137, 138, 141, 147, 150, 151, 153, 160
Mount Everest 10, 84

N

Nantucket 67, 68
National Child Welfare Association 63
New Orleans, Louisiana 34, 35, 37, 76
New Worlds to Conquer 21, 90, 91, 95, 96, 103, 105
Nicholas II of Russia 129
Novarro, Ramón 109, 111

O

Octorara 37
Odyssey, The 87
Olmsted, Frederick Law 39

P

Panama Canal 10, 91, 92, 93, 94, 122
Parkview Hotel 72, 73, 79, 80, 86
Patton, Francis Landly 42
Pickford, Mary 58, 67, 106, 125, 134
Potter, John 147, 150, 151, 152, 153
Princeton Pictorial 46, 50, 52
Princeton University 14, 27, 29, 31, 34, 36, 37, 39, 41, 42, 43, 44, 45, 46, 47, 49, 50, 52, 53, 54, 59, 61, 70, 71, 72, 74, 75, 79, 84, 87, 141, 164, 165, 166, 167

R

Rand, Ayn 137, 141
Rhodes College 160, 163, 164, 165

Richard Halliburton: The Story of His Life's Adventures 159
Royal Road to Romance, The 46, 47, 50, 61, 72, 74, 76, 79, 80, 81, 83, 87, 105, 166

S

Schuler, Loring 90, 91, 98, 106, 112
Sea Dragon 9, 14, 142, 143, 147, 149, 150, 151, 152, 153, 154, 155, 156
Seiberling, James Penfield "Shorty" 40, 46, 167
Seven League Boots 128, 132
Sheltering Arms Orphan Asylum 63, 64
Sinclair, Gordon 82, 149, 150, 152, 153
Smithsonian magazine 14
Steinbeck, John 134
Stephens, Moye 106, 107, 108, 109, 110, 112, 113, 114, 115, 116, 117, 118, 119, 120, 121, 123, 150, 167, 168
Sutherland, Abby 66
Swanson, Walter 144
Sweet, Channing "Chan" 40

T

Taft, William Howard 68
Taj Mahal 10, 55, 81, 82, 83, 84, 92, 114, 115, 149
Thomas, Lowell 84, 123
Torrey, Gordon 150, 151, 152, 153

U

Ulysses 72, 76, 87

W

Welch, John 147, 150
Wilson, Woodrow 42, 43
Wright, Frank Lloyd 104, 135, 136

About the Author

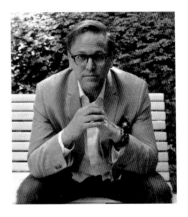

R. Scott Williams is an advertising, marketing and public relations executive with a passion for researching and recording unpublished stories of the early American South. After receiving his degree in journalism from the University of Memphis, he worked a variety of jobs until landing at Graceland, where he helped take care of business for the king for more than twelve years. Currently, he leads the marketing and communication initiatives at the Newseum, a museum of news and history in Washington, D.C. He resides in Arlington, Virginia, with his wife, Michelle, and daughters, Alex and Liv. In his spare time, Williams explores the historic sites around Washington, D.C., on his road bike and researches and records the lives of his West Tennessee ancestors.